THE NATURE OF DOCTRINE

THE NATURE OF DOCTRINE

Religion and Theology in a Postliberal Age

GEORGE A. LINDBECK

THE WESTMINSTER PRESS
Philadelphia

Book Design by Alice Derr

First edition

Published by The Westminster Press ®
Philadelphia, Pennsylvania

PRINTED IN THE UNITED STATES OF AMERICA
9 8 7 6 5 4 3 2 1

Library of Congress Cataloging in Publication Data

Lindbeck, George A.
  The nature of doctrine.

  Includes bibliographical references and index.
  1. Dogma. 2. Religion. 3. Religions. 4. Theology.
5. Christian union. I. Title.
BT19.L55 1984   230   83-27332
ISBN 0-664-21829-6
ISBN 0-664-24618-4 (pbk.)

CONTENTS

FOREWORD

This book is the product of a quarter century of growing dissatisfaction with the usual ways of thinking about those norms of communal belief and action which are generally spoken of as the doctrines or dogmas of churches. It has become apparent to me, during twenty-five years of involvement in ecumenical discussions and in teaching about the history and present status of doctrines, that those of us who are engaged in these activities lack adequate categories for conceptualizing the problems that arise. We are often unable, for example, to specify the criteria we implicitly employ when we say that some changes are faithful to a doctrinal tradition and others unfaithful, or some doctrinal differences are church-dividing and others not. Doctrines, in other words, do not behave the way they should, given our customary suppositions about the kinds of things they are. We clearly need new and better ways of understanding their nature and function.

The problem, as the title of this essay suggests, is not confined to doctrines per se, but extends to the notion of religion itself. Theories of religion and of doctrine are interdependent, and deficiencies in one area are inseparable from deficiencies in the other. Furthermore, all the standard theological approaches are unhelpful. The difficulties cannot be solved by, for example, abandoning modern developments and returning to some form of preliberal orthodoxy. A third, a postliberal, way of conceiving religion and religious doctrine is called for.

Although the focus of this book is on intra-Christian theological and ecumenical issues, the theory of religion and religious doctrine that it proposes is not specifically ecumenical, nor Christian, nor theological. It rather derives from philosophical and social-scientific approaches; and yet, so I shall argue, it has advantages, not only for the nontheological study of religion but also for Christian—and perhaps also non-Christian—ecumenical and theological purposes. What is new about the present work, in short, is not its theory of religion, but the use of this theory in the conceptualization of doctrine, and the contention that this conceptualization is fruitful for theology and ecumenism. The range of the argument extends uncomfortably far beyond the ecumenical concerns that prompted it, but this is inescapable. A theory of religion and doctrine cannot be ecumenically useful unless it is nonecumenically plausible.

Thus the following pages can be read in two different ways. They are on one level simply a contribution to the theory of religion and religious doctrine that may be of interest to both theological and nontheological students of Christianity as well as other faiths; but they are also intended as prolegomena to a book I have long been trying to write on the current status of the doctrinal agreements and disagreements of the major Christian traditions. The basic thesis, to repeat, presupposes no special ecumenical concerns on the part of the reader, and yet the ecumenical implications are developed in greater detail than would have been the case if the book were written by someone not engaged, as I have been, in efforts to overcome Christian divisions.

Before sketching the main feature of the proposed theory in the first chapter, it may be helpful in the remainder of this introduction to note some of the general characteristics of the argument. In origin, even if not always in presentation, this inquiry is very much a matter of seeking concepts that will remove anomalies. What I mean by this can be illustrated by a psychological experiment that, in the words of Thomas S. Kuhn, "deserves to be far better known outside the trade"[1]: Bruner and Postman introduced idiosyncratic combinations, such as a red six of spades and a black four of hearts, into a series of otherwise normal playing cards that experimental subjects were asked to identify in rapid succession. All the subjects initially perceived the anomalous cards incorrectly, but as exposure time was lengthened, they became confused. With further lengthening of exposure, most hit on the idea that this or that card was of the wrong color, and after this happened two or three times, they were quickly able properly to identify all the cards. "A few subjects, however, were never able to make the requisite adjustment of their categories. Even at forty times the average exposure required to recognize normal cards for what they were, more than 10 percent of the anomalous cards were not correctly identified. And the subjects who then failed often experienced acute personal distress. One of them exclaimed: 'I can't make the suit out, whatever it is. It didn't even look like a card that time. I don't know what color it is now or whether it's a spade or a heart. I'm not even sure now what a spade looks like. My God!' "[2]

Theologians sometimes behave similarly. Anomalies accumulate, old categories fail, and with luck or skill—both attributed by believers to grace—new concepts are found that better serve to account for the data. If they are not found, the consequences can be intellectually and religiously traumatic.

As has already been indicated, the anomalies that concern us have to do especially with the interrelationship of doctrinal permanence and change, conflict and compatibility, unity and disunity, and variety and uniformity among, but especially within, religions. Some of the questions involved in this set of problems have long been discussed under the rubric "development of doctrine,"[3] but puzzles have multiplied and become increasingly acute in recent times because of both ecumenical and interreligious trends and the proliferation of foundational, systematic, historical, and pastoral difficulties. As a result, the range of topics on which the present work touches is embarrassingly wide.

In order to limit the inquiry, therefore, it has been necessary to keep it strictly theoretical. No attempt is made to assess the reliability of the presumed facts about the doctrinal positions of the churches, which constitute the data with which we shall work. These data are taken hypothetically rather than assertorically: If such or such is the case, how can it be best understood? If some reality, like a card that doesn't look like a card, seems impossible, what concepts or theory can allow for its possibility? If, for example, doctrines are said to be "irreformable," as was said by Vatican I, what understanding of doctrine would make such a view intelligible without, however, excluding the contrary position? Or, to cite another illustration, are there ways of understanding apparently absurd claims of ecumenical agreement that grant that they may possibly be warranted, rather than insisting *a priori* that they must be mistaken? Whether they are in fact warranted, however, we shall leave to other and more directly ecumenical investigations.

As is appropriate in a theoretical inquiry more concerned with how to think than with what to assert about matters of fact, the proposals advanced in this book are intended to be acceptable to all religious traditions that fall within its purview. They are, in other words, meant to be ecumenically and religiously neutral. They do not in themselves imply decisions either for or against the communally authoritative teachings of particular religious bodies. This claim of doctrinal neutrality is later tested at some length in reference to classic Trinitarian and Christological affirmations, Marian dogmas, and infallibility. To the degree that the test is passed, the proposed approach may prove useful to both orthodox and unorthodox Christians, and to Catholics as well as Protestants. Nor does the suggested outlook prejudge the issue of whether Christianity or any other religion is right or wrong, and it might therefore be helpful to Christians in discussions with adherents of other religions or no religion at all. A different problem, little discussed in the following pages, is whether this outlook is also neutral from non-Christian perspectives. Some religions or quasi religions such as Hinduism, Buddhism, or Marxism—but not, I think, Judaism or Islam—may be implicitly committed to contrary theories of religion; but this question is best left to adherents of these other faiths. In any case, although the suggestions advanced in this book may not be universally utilizable, they seek, not to decide material questions, but to provide a framework for their discussion.

It would be a mistake, however, to suppose that this attempt at doctrinal neutrality involves theological neutrality when theology is understood as the scholarly activity of second-order reflection on the data of religion (including doctrinal data) and of formulating arguments for or against material positions (including doctrinal ones). Much, perhaps all, theology in this specific sense is to some degree implicitly or explicitly dependent on ideas derived from one or another theory of religion, and is therefore subject to criticism from contrary theoretical perspectives. The last chapter of this book discusses the way of doing theology that fits the proposed outlook. Whatever else might be said about it, the recommended mode is clearly in conflict both with traditionalist propositional orthodoxy and with currently regnant forms of liberalism.

This suggests, quite rightly, that the motivations for this book are ultimately more substantively theological than purely theoretical. As one who is deeply concerned about Christian unity, I would like to believe, as have most theologians down through the ages, that my work is of service to the church and to the glory of God. In brief, although the argument of the book is designed to be doctrinally and religiously neutral, it is prompted by convictions about the kind of theological thinking that is most likely to be religiously helpful to Christians and perhaps others in the present situation.

Motivations and convictions, however, have little to do with the strength of arguments. Even at best, the case for or against a comprehensive theory can only be suggestive rather than demonstrative. As is partly illustrated by the playing-card experiment, theoretical frameworks shape perceptions of problems and their possible solutions in such a way that each framework is in itself irrefutable. If, for example, some of the experimental subjects were fixated on explaining their confused perceptions in terms of their individual psychology or physiology, they would never ask whether the oddity of the cards themselves might be the source of their difficulties (or vice versa, if the problem were in fact psychological or physiological in origin). In a somewhat analogous and much more intractable way, each of the all-embracing and fundamentally different perspectives on religion and doctrine that we shall discuss has a particular view of what is relevant evidence for or against its own adequacy. Philosophers of science now often say that, even in the empirically most objective disciplines, all observation terms and all observation sentences are theory-laden. Even in physics and chemistry, "The adoption of a particular theory ordinarily alters the meaning of the observation terms, that is, alters the facts to be accounted for."[4] This point can be amply illustrated from the history of the shifts from Aristotelian, to Newtonian, to Einsteinian physics, but what applies in this domain is even more forcefully evident in theories of religion. There is no higher neutral standpoint from which to adjudicate their competing perceptions of what is factual and/or anomalous. Comprehensive outlooks on religion, not to mention religions themselves, are not susceptible to decisive confirmation or disconfirmation.

The case developed in this book, it should be noted, is circular rather than linear. Its persuasiveness, if any, does not depend on moving step by step in a demonstrative sequence, but on the illuminating power of the whole. It may be that if light dawns, it will be over the whole landscape simultaneously.[5] Thus the order of topics is in some respects optional: it would have been possible to start with the comments on theological method in the last chapter, or on infallibility in the fifth, rather than with the discussion of the possibility of doctrinal reconciliation in the first. Nevertheless, one must begin somewhere.

The place I have chosen to begin is first with ecumenism and second with current trends in theories of religion. This material is largely, though not entirely, descriptive and therefore, as befits the theoretical nature of the inquiry, hypothetical: if this is the character of the contemporary ecumenical situation and the wider intellectual, cultural, and religious context, then these are some of the ways in which theories of religion and doctrine may have practical import. The purpose of this exposition is to indicate some of the interrelationships of theory and praxis, not to insist on the adequacy of the description. Even if the characterization of present realities is inaccurate, the basic thesis may be valid.

The argument proper begins in Chapter 2 with a comparison of one of the currently influential theological theories of religion to the approach that this book proposes, and it concludes that the latter is superior at least for nontheological purposes. Chapter 3 takes up the question of theological viability. Can the proposed approach allow for the possible validity of the radically opposed claims made in the past and present by various religious traditions, regarding religious truth, falsity, and unsurpassability? What does the approach imply about the relationship between different religions, especially between Christianity and other religions? Does it permit rationales for interreligious dialogue that do not involve what for many believers is the impossible condition of surrendering exclusivist claims?

Chapters 4 and 5 test the compatibility of the approach with what some traditions hold regarding the permanence, change, and development of doctrines, and regarding the authority of the magisterial (teaching) office. These questions are discussed, as earlier mentioned, in reference to Christological and Trinitarian affirmations, Marian dogmas, and infallibility, but this is done to exemplify the doctrinal neutrality of the approach, not to decide material issues. These chapters are central for the ecumenical purposes of the book, but they also have implications for other areas.

Some of these implications for other areas are explored in the final chapter, which suggests that although there can be no single best theology (because what is best depends in part on the historical context), yet "dogmatic" methods are preferable to "apologetic" ones in constructive or systematic work, and stronger criteria can be formulated than are often supposed possible for distinguishing between legitimate and illegitimate (or orthodox and heterodox) developments and adaptations. Foundational theology, furthermore, changes its character and becomes less crucial than for many theologians, and apologetics becomes primarily a matter of appropriate communal praxis (in partial agreement with liberation theology, but with much more variable policy consequences). Finally, even if possibilities of theological collaboration and consensus were increased by the spread of the theory of religion and doctrine proposed in this essay, that would not guarantee that the possibilities would be exploited. In any case, new anomalies might develop to replace the old; and yet that is not a reason for clinging to old problems rather than taking the risk of confronting new ones.

Portions of the first five of the following six chapters derive from the St. Michael's Lectures delivered in the fall of 1974 at Gonzaga University. Although the present investigation does not focus primarily on the questions of doctrinal permanence and infallibility, as did those lectures, and although only traces remain of the extensive discussions of Bernard Lonergan,[6] yet there is a substantial overlap.

On the other hand, the changes are large enough to make it inadvisable to include the questions and answers evoked by the lectures when they were originally delivered. I learned much from those exchanges. They suggested ideas that have since been incorporated into my own thinking, and I wish it were possible properly to identify and acknowledge all that I owe both to those who so generously gave of their time and attention when I first broached some of the themes discussed in the following pages and to those, students and colleagues at Yale and elsewhere, who have since read successive drafts and given me the benefit of their reflections. At least a dozen names would have to be mentioned from this latter group alone (and even then the list would be incomplete), but one name at least must be mentioned, that of Hans Frei. I owe more than I can tell both to his encouragement and to his thought. Special appreciation must also be expressed to Father William F. J. Ryan, S.J., and Father Patrick O'Leary, S.J., who started this book on its way by inviting me to give the St. Michael's Lectures and then urged me to prepare them for publication. I hope they will be able to view this offspring of their invitation as in some measure a recompense for their long wait.

NOTES

1. Thomas S. Kuhn, *The Structure of Scientific Revolutions,* 2d ed. (University of Chicago Press, 1970), p. 62.

2. Ibid., pp. 63–64.

3. The rubric "development of doctrine" has been in use since John Henry Newman, *An Essay on the Development of Christian Doctrine,* 1st ed. (London, 1845).

4. Ernan McMullin, "The Two Faces of Science," *Review of Metaphysics,* Vol. 27 (1974), p. 663.

5. Ludwig Wittgenstein, *On Certainty* (Oxford: Basil Blackwell, 1969), #105.

6. See esp. pp. 31–32, 94, below.

CHAPTER 1

THEORY, ECUMENISM, AND CULTURE: THE PROPOSAL IN CONTEXT

I
THE ECUMENICAL MATRIX

Over and over again in recent years, there have been reports from Roman Catholic, Orthodox, or Protestant theologians engaged in dialogues sponsored by their respective churches that they are in basic agreement on such topics as the Eucharist, ministry, justification, or even the papacy, and yet they continue—so they claim—to adhere to their historic and once-divisive convictions.[1] Those who hear these reports often find them difficult to believe. They are inclined to think that the very notion of doctrinal reconciliation without doctrinal change is self-contradictory, and they suspect that the dialogue participants are self-deceived victims of their desire to combine ecumenical harmony with denominational loyalty. The dialogue members (including the author of these pages) usually protest. They say they have been compelled by the evidence, sometimes against their earlier inclinations, to conclude that positions that were once really opposed are now really reconcilable, even though these positions remain in a significant sense identical to what they were before.[2]

If one credits these testimonies, the problem is not with the reality but with the comprehensibility of this strange combination of constancy and change, unity and diversity. The proper response in that case is not to deny the reality on the grounds that it seems impossible, but rather to seek to explain its possibility. If adequate concepts for conceptualizing this possibility are not available, better ones should be sought. Believers may quite rightly account on one level for reconcilability by appealing to mystery, to the power of the Holy Spirit, but they ought not do so in such a way as to terminate the quest for a more mundane kind of intelligibility. That, at any rate, is the conviction of those who believe that theology is *fides quaerens intellectum* (faith seeking understanding), and that its practitioners are therefore obligated to try to untie intellectual knots by intellectual means.

The effort to follow this precept in reference to our present problem suffers, however, from the handicap of working with views of doctrine and religion that were forged in other circumstances to deal with other difficulties. The contemporary ecumenical problematic was not their concern. Much more will be said of these approaches later, but the time has now come briefly to introduce them.

The currently most familiar theological theories of religion and doctrine can, for our purposes, be divided into three types. One of these emphasizes the cognitive aspects of religion and stresses the ways in which church doctrines function as informative propositions or truth claims about objective realities. Religions are thus thought of as similar to philosophy or science as these were classically conceived. This was the approach of traditional orthodoxies (as well as of many heterodoxies), but it also has certain affinities to the outlook on religion adopted by much modern Anglo-American analytic philosophy with its preoccupation with the cognitive or informational meaningfulness of religious utterances. A second approach focuses on what I shall call in this book the "experiential-expressive" dimension of religion, and it interprets doctrines as noninformative and nondiscursive symbols of inner feelings, attitudes, or existential orientations. This approach highlights the resemblances of religions to aesthetic enterprises and is particularly congenial to the liberal theologies influenced by the Continental developments that began with Schleiermacher. A third approach, favored especially by ecumenically inclined Roman Catholics, attempts to combine these two emphases. Both the cognitively propositional and the expressively symbolic dimensions and functions of religion and doctrine are viewed, at least in the case of Christianity, as religiously significant and valid. Karl Rahner and Bernard Lonergan have developed what are probably the currently most influential versions of this two-dimensional outlook. Like many hybrids, this outlook has advantages over one-dimensional alternatives, but for our purposes it will generally be subsumed under the earlier approaches.

In all of these perspectives it is difficult to envision the possibility of doctrinal reconciliation without capitulation. Indeed, in the first two the possibility is simply denied: either doctrinal reconciliation or constancy must be rejected. For a propositionalist, if a doctrine is once true, it is always true, and if it is once false, it is always false.[3] This implies, for example, that the historic affirmations and denials of transubstantiation can never be harmonized. Agreement can be reached only if one or both sides abandon their earlier positions. Thus, on this view, doctrinal reconciliation without capitulation is impossible because there is no significant sense in which the meaning of a doctrine can change while remaining the same.

For experiential-expressive symbolists, in contrast, religiously significant meanings can vary while doctrines remain the same, and conversely, doctrines can alter without change of meaning. Both transubstantiationist and nontransubstantiationist conceptualities—to continue with the previous example—can express or evoke similar or dissimilar experiences of divine reality, or no experience at all. The general principle is that insofar as doctrines function as nondiscursive symbols, they are polyvalent in import and therefore subject to changes of meaning or even to a total loss of meaningfulness, to what Tillich calls their death.[4] They are not crucial for religious agreement or disagreement, because these are constituted by harmony or conflict in underlying feelings, attitudes, existential orientations, or practices, rather than by what happens on the level of symbolic (including doctrinal) objectifications. There is thus at least the logical possibility that a Buddhist and a Christian might have basically the same faith, although expressed very differently.

Theories of the third type, which utilize both cognitivist and experiential-expressive perspectives, are equipped to account more fully than can the first two types for both variable and invariable aspects of religious traditions but have difficulty in coherently combining them. Even at their best, as in Rahner and Lonergan, they resort to complicated intellectual gymnastics and to that extent are unpersuasive. They are also weak in criteria for determining when a given doctrinal development is consistent with the sources of faith, and they are therefore unable to avoid a rather greater reliance on the magisterium, the official teaching authority of the church, for decisions in such matters than all Reformation Protestants and many Catholics consider desirable. In short, although two-dimensional views are superior for ecumenical purposes in that they do not *a priori* exclude doctrinal reconciliation without capitulation as do simple propositionalism and simple symbolism, yet their explanations of how this is possible tend to be too awkward and complex to be easily intelligible or convincing.[5] There would be less skepticism about ecumenical claims if it were possible to find an alternative approach that made the intertwining of variability and invariability in matters of faith easier to understand.

This book proposes such an alternative. The elements of this approach are relatively recent but not unfamiliar, and yet they have been neglected by theologians when dealing with anomalies such as the one with which we are now struggling. It has become customary in a considerable body of anthropological, sociological, and philosophical literature (about which more will be said later) to emphasize neither the cognitive nor the experiential-expressive aspects of religion; rather, emphasis is placed on those respects in which religions resemble languages together with their correlative forms of life and are thus similar to cultures (insofar as these are understood semiotically as reality and value systems—that is, as idioms for the construing of reality and the living of life). The function of church doctrines that becomes most prominent in this perspective is their use, not as expressive symbols or as truth claims, but as communally authoritative rules of discourse, attitude, and action. This general way of conceptualizing religion will be called in what follows a "cultural-linguistic" approach, and the implied view of church doctrine will be referred to as a "regulative" or "rule" theory.

A regulative approach has no difficulty explaining the possibility of reconciliation without capitulation. Rules, unlike propositions or expressive symbols, retain an invariant meaning under changing conditions of compatibility and conflict. For example, the rules "Drive on the left" and "Drive on the right" are unequivocal in meaning and unequivocally opposed, yet both may be binding: one in Britain and the other in the United States, or one when traffic is normal, and the other when a collision must be avoided. Thus oppositions between rules can in some instances be resolved, not by altering one or both of them, but by specifying when or where they apply, or by stipulating which of the competing directives takes precedence. Similarly, to return to the eucharistic example, both transubstantiation and at least some of the doctrines that appear to contradict it can be interpreted as embodying rules of sacramental thought and practice that may have been in unavoidable and perhaps irresolvable collision in certain historical contexts, but that can in other circumstances be harmonized by appropriate specifications of their respective domains, uses, and priorities. In short, to the degree that doctrines function as rules, as we shall see in more detail in Chapter 4, there is no logical problem in understanding how historically opposed positions can in some, even if not all, cases be reconciled while remaining in themselves unchanged. Contrary to what happens when doctrines are construed as propositions or expressive symbols, doctrinal reconciliation without capitulation is a coherent notion.

It could be shown that this account approximates a pattern of reasoning often found in ecumenical agreements, not least on the Lord's Supper. Doctrines may be talked about in these agreements as if they were propositions or, in some cases, nondiscursive symbols, but they are treated as if they were rules or regulative principles.[6]

The insight that church doctrines resemble rules, it should next be noted, is not novel. The notion of *regulae fidei* goes back to the earliest Christian centuries, and later historians and systematic theologians have often recognized in varying degrees that the operational logic of religious teachings in their communally authoritative (or, as we shall simply say, doctrinal) role is regulative. They have recognized, in other words, that at least part of the task of doctrines is to recommend and exclude certain ranges of—among other things—propositional utterances or symbolizing activities.[7] What is innovative about the present proposal is that this becomes the only job that doctrines do in their role as church teachings.

This is not to suggest that other functions of doctrinal formulations are unimportant. The chanting of the Nicene Creed, as Tolstoy observed with puzzlement among Russian peasants,[8] can be an immensely powerful symbolization of the totality of the faith even for those who do not understand its discursive propositional or regulative meanings. There are other Christians, however, for whom the expressively symbolic or liturgical role of the Nicaenum is minimal and for whom it is nevertheless of the utmost doctrinal importance. Old-style Calvinists, for example, did not sing it in their eucharistic celebrations, but it was for them a crucial means for differentiating themselves from Unitarians. They used it, one might say, doctrinally but not symbolically.

Admittedly it is not equally obvious that a creed may function regulatively (doctrinally) and yet not propositionally. It seems odd to suggest that the Nicaenum in its role as a communal doctrine does not make first-order truth claims, and yet this is what I shall contend. Doctrines regulate truth claims by excluding some and permitting others, but the logic of their communally authoritative use hinders or prevents them from specifying positively what is to be affirmed.

This, however, is to anticipate: further discussion of this issue must be postponed. We have now said enough to indicate the ecumenical bearing of a cultural-linguistic approach to religion and of a regulative view of doctrine and can therefore turn to the place of this approach among contemporary trends in theory of religion.

II
THE PSYCHOSOCIAL CONTEXT

In modern times, propositional understandings of religion have long been on the defensive and experiential-expressive ones in the ascendency. Cultural-linguistic approaches are the most recent arrivals on the scene, but while increasingly common in nontheological religious studies, they have on the whole been neglected by those who are religiously interested in religion. In this section we shall ask why this is so. Our concern will be with historical and psychosocial causes of the religious and theological attractiveness of experiential expressivism in contrast to a cultural-linguistic outlook, but with the understanding that causal considerations do not settle the question of truth or rightness. The situational pressures in favor of looking at religion one way rather than another may be tremendous, but that by itself does not decide the issue of empirical, conceptual, or theological adequacy. It is possible that modernity conditions the religiously concerned to favor ways of viewing religion that are in general more satisfactory than the alternatives just as, on an evolutionary model, natural selection ensures that most human beings see the world in a more richly differentiated and informative manner than do the color-blind; but then, perhaps it is the moderns who suffer from culturally induced scotoma in matters religious.[9] No attempt is being made to pronounce on this issue at the present stage of the argument; the purpose here is simply to sketch the nature of the conditioning.

Some of the conditioning factors that favor experiential-expressivism are intrinsic to our cultural and social situation, while others are relatively accidental. Among the latter factors is the novelty of the cultural-linguistic alternative. Although its roots go back on the cultural side to Marx, Weber, and Durkheim,[10] and on the linguistic side to Wittgenstein,[11] it is only rarely and recently that it has become a programmatic approach to the study of religion, as, for instance, in the philosopher Peter Winch[12] and the anthropologist Clifford Geertz,[13] Other authors who have contributed to the understanding in this book of a cultural and/or linguistic outlook on religion (even if under other names) are the sociologist of knowledge Peter Berger[14] and the critical philosophers of religion Ninian Smart[15] and William Christian;[16] but again, their works are the products of recent decades, and in these particular cases the theories are self-consciously nontheological. Peter Berger is particularly interesting in this latter respect, for in his cultural model of religion[17] he is, by his own avowal, "methodologically atheistic," but when he writes an apologetic for religion, his theory is basically experiential-expressivist with strong affinities to that of Schleiermacher.[18] It may be that Berger has failed to make theological use of his own cultural theory, not because it is intrinsically unusable for religious purposes (as he appears to assume that it is), but because it belongs to a way of thinking about religion that has heretofore scarcely ever been employed except "atheistically."

This, however, even if true, is an incomplete explanation of the neglect. Contemporary thinkers are not simply deterred by the inherent difficulties of using concepts in untested ways for unfamiliar purposes; they are, on the positive side, also attracted by the powerful conceptualities developed in a long and notable experiential tradition.[19] The origins of this tradition in one sense go back to Kant, for he helped clear the ground for its emergence by demolishing the metaphysical and epistemological foundations of the earlier regnant cognitive-propositional views. That ground-clearing was later completed for most educated people by scientific developments that increased the difficulties of accepting literalistic propositional interpretations of such biblical doctrines as creation, and by historical studies that implied the time-conditioned relativity of all doctrines. Kant, however, did not replace the view of religion he had undermined with a more adequate one. His reduction of God to a transcendental condition (albeit a necessary one) of morality seemed to the sensibilities of most religious people to leave religion intolerably impoverished. The breach was filled, beginning with Schleiermacher, with what I have called "experiential-expressivism," but this comes in many varieties and can be given many names. In Schleiermacher's case, it will be recalled, the source of all religion is in the "feeling of absolute dependence,"[20] but there are many and significantly different ways of describing the basic religious experience, as is illustrated by a succession of influential theories of religion stretching from Schleiermacher through Rudolf Otto to Mircea Eliade and beyond. Nevertheless, whatever the variations, thinkers of this tradition all locate ultimately significant contact with whatever is finally important to religion in the prereflective experiential depths of the self and regard the public or outer features of religion as expressive and evocative objectifications (i.e., nondiscursive symbols) of internal experience. For nearly two hundred years this tradition has provided intellectually brilliant and empirically impressive accounts of the religious life that have been compatible with—indeed, often at the heart of —the romantic, idealistic, and phenomenological-existentialist streams of thought that have dominated the humanistic side of Western culture ever since Kant's revolutionary Copernican "turn to the subject."[21] So weighty a heritage should not be jettisoned except for good reasons; but even if there are good reasons, it is difficult to abandon. The habits of thought it has fostered are ingrained in the soul of the modern West, perhaps particularly in the souls of theologians.

Yet the struggle is not simply between newness, on the one side, and the force of habit, on the other: there are also psychosocial pressures that work against cultural-linguistic approaches and in favor of experiential-expressive ones. One way of characterizing the basic problem is to speak, as Thomas Luckmann and Peter Berger have done, of that "deobjectification" of religion and doctrine which, from the perspective of the sociology of knowledge, is an inescapable consequence of the individualism, rapid change, and religious pluralism of modern societies.[22] This deobjectification occurs quite apart from the experiential theories that supply its intellectual backing. Fewer and fewer contemporary people are deeply embedded in particular religious traditions or thoroughly involved in particular religious communities. This makes it hard for them to perceive or experience religion in cognitivist fashion as the acceptance of sets of objectively and immutably true propositions. Perhaps only those among whom the sects chiefly recruit who combine unusual insecurity with naiveté can easily manage to do this.

These same factors, however, also create difficulties for thinking of the process of becoming religious as similar to that of acquiring a culture or learning a language—that is, interiorizing outlooks that others have created, and mastering skills that others have honed. The mere idea that becoming religious might on occasion be rather like achieving competence in the totally nonoptional grammatical patterns and lexical resources of a foreign tongue seems alienating and oppressive, an infringement of freedom and choice, a denial of creativity, and repugnant to all the most cherished values of modernity. It is much easier in our day for religious interests to take the experiential-expressive form of individual quests for personal meaning. This is true even among theological conservatives, as is illustrated by the stress placed on conversion experiences by the heirs of pietism and revivalism. The structures of modernity press individuals to meet God first in the depths of their souls and then, perhaps, if they find something personally congenial, to become part of a tradition or join a church. Their actual behavior may not conform to this model, but it is the way they experience themselves. Thus the traditions of religious thought and practice into which Westerners are most likely to be socialized conceals from them the social origins of their conviction that religion is a highly private and individual matter.

This pattern was already well established in American Protestantism by the nineteenth century, but in the past both conservatives and liberals generally thought of the search for individual religious meaning as taking place within the capacious confines of the many varieties of Christianity. As we move into a culturally (even if not statistically) post-Christian period, however, increasing numbers of people regard all religions as possible sources of symbols to be used eclectically in articulating, clarifying, and organizing the experiences of the inner self. Religions are seen as multiple suppliers of different forms of a single commodity needed for transcendent self-expression and self-realization. Theologians, ministers, and perhaps above all teachers of religion in colleges and universities whose job is to meet the demand are under great pressure in these circumstances to emphasize the experiential-expressive aspects of religion. It is thus that they can most easily market it.[23]

Cultural appeal does not in this context, however, necessarily imply mediocrity. There are authors of admirable quality, such as Mircea Eliade, Thomas Campbell, and John S. Dunne, who have done estimable work in making the symbolic resources of the world's religions available to the interested. Further, we must remember that the appetite for materials with which to construct a personal religious vision springs from deeply rooted needs for meaning, order, and transcendence and can take noble as well as vulgar forms. Finally, the theologians whose work is shaped by the desire to meet these needs are often fully aware that religion is inseparable from particular traditions and communities. They often do not share the Whiteheadian (and Plotinian) view that "religion is what the individual does with his own solitariness,"[24] although they may well assent to the quite different proposition that what we do with our solitude is crucially affected by religion. Nevertheless, the exigencies of communicating their messages in a privatistic cultural and social milieu lead them to commend public and communal traditions as optional aids in individual self-realization rather than as bearers of normative realities to be interiorized.

A further cause for the attractiveness of experiential-expressive models is likely to seem objectively more compelling to some readers. Such models are particularly well fitted to supply a rationale for the interreligious dialogue and cooperation that is so urgently needed in a divided yet shrinking world. The rationale suggested, though not necessitated, by an experiential-expressive approach is that the various religions are diverse symbolizations of one and the same core experience of the Ultimate, and that therefore they must respect each other, learn from each other, and reciprocally enrich each other. According to some versions of this approach, they can be expected to converge more and more.[25] In a cultural-linguistic outlook, in contrast, it is just as hard to think of religions as it is to think of cultures or languages as having a single generic or universal experiential essence of which particular religions—or cultures or languages—are varied manifestations or modifications. One can in this outlook no more be religious in general than one can speak language in general.[26] Thus the focus is on particular religions rather than on religious universals and their combinations and permutations. The results of this particularity may be useful for the restrictedly ecumenical end of promoting unity within a single religion, but not for the broader purpose of seeking the unity of all religions.

In addition to these psychosocial considerations, there are also apparent theoretical or conceptual difficulties working against the religious or theological use of cultural-linguistic approaches and thus by default favoring experiential-expressive ones. One problem is that languages and cultures do not make truth claims, are relative to particular times and places, and are difficult to think of as having transcendent rather than this-worldly origins. They seem ill fitted to serve as analogues for religions such as Christianity, which, as traditionally interpreted, claim to be true, universally valid, and supernaturally revealed. Clearly old-fashioned propositional theories that liken a religion to a science or a philosophy, as these were classically understood, seems better fitted to account for these religious claims, but experiential-expressive models can also be easily adapted for this purpose. The depth experiences in which religions originate according to expressive models are easily pictured as involving communion with or openness to transcendent reality, and this makes it possible to speak of religions as having a certain kind of divine truth and, in their generic aspect, universal validity. Cultures and languages, in contrast, seem to most people, at least in our day, much more this-worldly than do the depth experiences of the inner self. No wonder, then, that those interested in commending religion to society at large have for the most part in recent times appealed to some form of inwardness as the source and center of authentic religiousness.

There are, to be sure, countervailing tendencies. Classical propositionalism, for example, is by no means dead or wholly discredited. There are thinkers of great contemporary philosophical sophistication, such as Peter Geach,[27] who emphasize the cognitive dimension of religion (or at least Christianity), and for whom church doctrines are first of all truth claims about objective realities. Traditionalists of this kind are by no means ignorant of modernity and are often among its most effective critics. Three of the best-known popular apologists of the century, G. K. Chesterton, C. S. Lewis, and Malcolm Muggeridge, although of varying degrees of orthodoxy, are clearly cognitivist in their view of religion and doctrine. Second, one strand in the so-called neo-orthodox movement, that of Barth (unlike Tillich's or Bultmann's), avoids the experiential-expressive turn to the subject. (There may also be other parallels between Barth's method and a cultural-linguistic approach, as will be briefly suggested in the last chapter.) Third, Wittgenstein's influence has been strong in some theological circles. While this does not appear to have yet inspired consideration of the problems of doctrinal constancy and change and of agreement and disagreement with which this book is concerned, it has served as a major stimulus to my thinking (even if in ways that those more knowledgeable in Wittgenstein might not approve).[28]

As was already suggested in the previous section, however, the major current alternative to one-dimensional experiential-expressive views of doctrine is provided by Roman Catholics such as Rahner and Lonergan. They accept the Kantian turn to the subject and the modern awareness of cultural and historical relativity, and they agree that this requires some form of experiential expressivism. Yet they also argue that this by itself is not able to account for the enduring self-identity and unity claimed by some religions, and they therefore postulate that there is, in addition to what Rahner calls the "transcendental" experiential and revelatory source of all religion, a "categorial" (and in part propositional) revelatory source of at least some religion. On this view, all religions have a measure of expressive revealed truth, but only those which are accepted as abidingly normative (e.g., biblical ones) would be regarded as having, in addition, propositional truth.[29] Whatever the difficulties of this approach, it has generated the most comprehensive efforts hitherto made to reconcile modern and traditional ways of conceptualizing religion and religious doctrine and must therefore be taken seriously by anyone who takes another road. Lonergan in particular has proved influential on the following chapters.

Yet, whatever the countervailing tendencies, the most significant development in theories of religion is the growing gap between theological and nontheological approaches. Experiential-expressivism has lost ground everywhere except in most theological schools and departments of religious studies where, if anything, the trend is the reverse.[30] Historians, anthropologists, sociologists, and philosophers (with the exception of some phenomenologists) seem increasingly to find cultural-linguistic approaches congenial. The reason for this gap appears to be that experiential expressivism fits the religious needs of modernity, while (as we shall later try to explain in more detail) cultural and linguistic approaches are better suited to the nontheological study of religion.

This scholarly ascendancy of cultural and linguistic approaches, it should be noted, is not confined to the study of religion. Rather, it characterizes the human sciences in general when dealing with nonreligious no less than religious phenomena. We have already spoken of historians, anthropologists, sociologists, and philosophers as influenced by this trend, but one could also mention psychologists among whom attribution theory is of growing importance.[31] Subfields as well as larger disciplines have been affected. In criminology, to cite an illustration at random, there has been a clearly marked development from nineteenth-century concentration on individual character traits, through phases in which social, economic, and psychological factors preoccupied the scholars, to the contemporary tendency to give increasing attention to cultural definitions of the good and the bad, the real and the unreal, the deviant and the normal.[32] It is to be expected that parallel developments would take place in the study of religion insofar as this study is independent of specifically religious interests.

Whether this development is good or bad must at this point be left an open question. Obviously there are disadvantages in the growing isolation of the religiously interested study of religion from some of the most fruitful intellectual currents of the day. It tends to ghettoize theology and deprives it of the vitality that comes from close association with the best in nontheological thinking. On the other hand, experiential expressivism would seem to be so "relevant," so suited to contemporary sensibilities, that the nontheological and theological cases for the superiority of cultural and linguistic approaches must be very strong indeed before these approaches to religion and doctrine have much chance of being adopted. It is to these cases that we now turn in the next two chapters.

NOTES

1. The summary of dialogue results given in N. Ehrenström and G. Gassmann, *Confessions in Dialogue: A Survey of Bilateral Conversations Among World Confessional Families, 1959–1974,* 3d ed. (Geneva: World Council of Churches, 1975), is complete up to the date of publication, but considerable additional material has since appeared. My own involvement has been chiefly in Roman Catholic/Lutheran discussions on the national and international levels, and I have contributed essays and prefaces or been otherwise involved in the preparation of the following: Lutherans and Catholics in Dialogue, 7 vols.: 1. *The Status of the Nicene Creed as Dogma of the Church* (1965); 2. *One Baptism for the Remission of Sins* (1966); 3. *The Eucharist as Sacrifice* (1967); 4. *Eucharist and Ministry* (1970); 5. *Papal Primacy and the Universal Church* (Augsburg Publishing House, 1974); 6. *Teaching Authority and Infallibility in the Church* (Augsburg Publishing House, 1980); 7. *Justification By Faith* (*Origins* 13 [Oct. 6, 1983], pp. 277–304). Vols. 1–4 were originally published by the Bishops' Committee for Ecumenical and Interreligious Affairs, Washington, D.C., and the U.S.A. National Committee of the Lutheran World Federation, New York, N.Y. Vols. 1–3 have been reprinted together by Augsburg Publishing House, and also Vol. 4.

Reports of the Joint Lutheran/Roman Catholic Commission of the Lutheran World Federation and the Vatican Secretariat for Promoting Christian Unity: "The Gospel and the Church," *Worship* 46 (1972), pp. 326–351, and *Lutheran World* 19 (1972), pp. 259–273. The text in German and English together with position papers are in H. Meyer (ed.), *Evangelium—Welt—Kirche: Schlussbericht and Referate der römisch-katholisch/evangelisch-lutherischen Studienkommission "Das Evangelium und die Kirche," 1967–1971* (Frankfurt: O. Lembeck/J. Knecht, 1975); *The Eucharist* (1980); *The Ministry in the Church* (1981). (The two latter items are published by the Lutheran World Federation, 150 Route de Ferney, CH-1211 Geneva 20, Switzerland.)

2. An independent evaluation of some of these dialogues is contained in "The Bilateral Consultations Between the Roman Catholic Church in the United States and Other Christian Communions: A Theological Review and Critique by the Study Committee Commissioned by the Board of Directors of the Catholic Theological Society of America" (1972), *Proceedings of the Catholic Theological Association of America* (1972), pp. 179–232.

3. This view of propositions is the focus of Hans Küng's attack on the doctrine of infallibility. See his *Infallible? An Inquiry,* tr. by Edward Quinn (Doubleday & Co., 1971), pp. 157–173.

4. Paul Tillich, *Systematic Theology,* Vol. 1 (University of Chicago Press, 1951), p. 240.

5. I have discussed aspects of Rahner's theory of development in "Reform and Infallibility," *Cross Currents* 11 (1961), pp. 345–356, and in "The Problem of Doctrinal Development and Contemporary Protestant Theology," E. Schillebeeckx and B. Willems (eds.), *Man as Man and Believer,* Concilium 21 (Paulist Press, 1967), pp. 133–146. I have discussed Lonergan's theory in "Protestant Problems

with Lonergan on the Development of Dogma," Philip McShane (ed.), *Foundations of Theology* (Dublin: Gill & Macmillan, 1971), pp. 115–124. In none of these instances, however, do I focus on the difficulties that now seem to me paramount.

6. This is not the book in which to argue this point in detail, but if I were to do so, I would make use of data such as that provided by the two reports on the Eucharist listed in n. 1, above.

7. One good contemporary example of this is Karl Rahner, "Pluralism in Theology and the Unity of the Creed in the Church," in his *Theological Investigations,* Vol. 11 (Seabury Press, 1974), pp. 3–23, esp. 14ff.

8. For Tolstoy's brief attempt to practice the religion of the muzhik, see N. Weisbein, *L' évolution religieuse de Tolstoi* (Paris: Cinq Continents, 1960), pp. 140–145.

9. This point is developed in the *Cross Currents* article referred to in n. 5, above.

10. Marx utilized a Hegelian dialectic to emphasize that human beings are themselves the products of what they produce; Max Weber, the specifically cultural (i.e., meaningful or significatory) character of social products and processes; Emile Durkheim, the objectivity of socially constructed reality (the state, for example, is experienced as no less objective and, for most purposes, much more important than mountains); and—to add to the list—G. H. Mead stressed the constitution of personal identity by the internalization of social reality. Religion, whatever else it may be or do, provides an overarching integrating and legitimating frame of reference for the socially constructed worlds that human beings inhabit. For this way of describing the general characteristics of a cultural view of religion I am indebted to Peter Berger and Thomas Luckmann, *The Social Construction of Reality* (Doubleday & Co., 1966), and to the more succinct statement in the first two chapters of Peter Berger, *The Sacred Canopy: Elements of a Sociological Theory of Religion* (Doubleday & Co., 1967).

11. W. D. Hudson, *Wittgenstein and Religious Belief* (London: Macmillan & Co., 1975).

12. Peter Winch, *The Idea of a Social Science and Its Relation to Philosophy* (London: Routledge & Kegan Paul, 1958); "Understanding a Primitive Society," in his *Ethics and Action* (London: Routledge & Kegan Paul, 1972); "Language, Belief and Relativism," in *Contemporary British Philosophy: Personal Statements*, ed. by H. D. Lewis (London: George Allen & Unwin, 1976).

13. Clifford Geertz, "Religion as a Cultural System," in his *The Interpretation of Cultures* (Basic Books, 1973), pp. 87–125.

14. See n. 10, above.

15. Ninian Smart, *Reasons and Faiths* (London: Routledge & Kegan Paul, 1958).

16. William A. Christian, Sr., *Meaning and Truth in Religion* (Princeton University Press, 1964); *Oppositions of Religious Doctrines* (Herder & Herder, 1972). Christian's concern to analyze the internal logic of schemes of religious doctrines is parallel, though not identical, to Geertz's interest in religions as similar to semiotic (or, less precisely, linguistic) systems. In both cases, attention focuses primarily on —in Geertz's terminology—"an analysis of the system of meanings embodied in the symbols which make up the religion proper" (*The Interpretation of Cultures,* p.

125). Another task, that of "relating these systems to social-structural and psychological processes" (ibid.) cannot be properly carried out unless the first is seriously pursued. It is this relatively greater emphasis on the internal logic or grammar of religions which differentiates what I am calling "cultural-linguistic" approaches to religion from more one-sidedly cultural ones. For another author with an approach similar to Christian's, see J. M. Bochenski, *The Logic of Religion* (New York University Press, 1965). Cf. William A. Christian, Sr., "Bochenski on the Structure of Schemes of Doctrines," *Religious Studies* 13 (1977), pp. 203–219.

17. See the works cited in n. 10, above.

18. Peter Berger specifically aligns himself with Schleiermacher in *The Heretical Imperative: Contemporary Possibilities of Religious Affirmation* (Doubleday & Co., 1980), p. 166. See also his *Rumor of Angels: Modern Society and the Rediscovery of the Supernatural* (Doubleday & Co., 1969).

19. One lively brief account of the liberal experiential-expressive tradition stemming from Schleiermacher is in Berger, *The Heretical Imperative*, pp. 114–142.

20. Friedrich Schleiermacher, *The Christian Faith* (Edinburgh: T. & T. Clark, 1928), #4.4, pp. 16–18.

21. For this phrase, see Bernard Lonergan, *The Subject* (Marquette University Press, 1968).

22. In addition to the works cited in nn. 10 and 18, above, see Thomas Luckmann, *The Invisible Religion* (Macmillan Co., 1967). Cf. also my articles "Ecumenism and the Future of Belief," *Una Sancta* 25/3 (1968), pp. 3–18; and "The Sectarian Future of the Church," in Joseph P. Whelan (ed.), *The God Experience* (Newman Press, 1971), pp. 226–243.

23. For the notion of religion as a marketable commodity, see Berger, *The Sacred Canopy*, pp. 137f.

24. Alfred North Whitehead, *Religion in the Making* (Macmillan Co., 1926), p. 16.

25. This view is not directly entailed by an experiential-expressive approach. It is possible to hold that some religions may be divergent rather than convergent in their depth dimensions. Most phenomenologically oriented theoreticians of religion, however, emphasize convergence. See, e.g., the brief discussions of Rudolf Otto, Joachim Wach, Mircea Eliade, and Wilfred Cantwell Smith in Ninian Smart, *The Science of Religion and the Sociology of Knowledge* (Princeton University Press, 1973).

26. This is a paraphrase of a remark of Santayana's cited without exact reference by Geertz, *The Interpretation of Cultures*, p. 87.

27. See, e.g., Peter Geach, *Providence and Evil* (Cambridge University Press, 1977).

28. I am particularly indebted to my colleague Paul Holmer for his understanding of what is theologically important about Wittgenstein. Some sense of the lessons he has tried to convey over the years is provided by his essay "Wittgenstein and Theology," in D. M. High (ed.), *New Essays on Religious Language* (New York: Oxford University Press, 1969).

29. Karl Rahner, "Christianity and Non-Christian Religions," in his *Theological*

Investigations, Vol. 5 (Seabury Press, 1966), pp. 115–134. For a brief presentation of the distinction between transcendental and categorial revelation, see especially Karl Rahner and Joseph Ratzinger, *Revelation and Tradition* (Herder & Herder, 1966), pp. 9–25.

30. I have elsewhere discussed the growing dominance in North America of "generic" approaches (which for the most part use experiential-expressive models) to the study of religion. See *University Divinity Schools: A Report on Ecclesiastically Independent Theological Education* (Rockefeller Foundation, 1976), esp. pp. 1–6, 35–41.

31. An accumulating body of experimental evidence indicates that unusual physiological states (such as might be induced, for example, by an injection of adrenalin) are experienced in terms of very different emotions (e.g., love, hate, jealousy, joy), depending on the cause to which the diffuse physical feeling is attributed (or, in other words, depending on the interpretive concepts that are employed). See Wayne Proudfoot, "Attribution Theory and the Psychology of Religion," *Journal for the Scientific Study of Religion* 14 (1975), pp. 317–330. A forthcoming book by the same author expands on the significance of attribution theory for the understanding of religious experience and, in my view, greatly strengthens the argument of the next chapter.

32. Marvin E. Wolfgang, "Real and Perceived Changes of Crime and Punishment," *Daedalus* 107/1 (1978), pp. 143–157, esp. 149–151.

CHAPTER 2

RELIGION AND EXPERIENCE:
A PRETHEOLOGICAL INQUIRY

The task of this chapter, it will be recalled, is to explore the nontheological case for a cultural-linguistic approach to religion and religious doctrines. What are the advantages of this outlook over cognitivist and experiential-expressive ways of picturing the phenomena? This question needs to be addressed before we deal, in the next chapter, with the theological issues raised by what we have already noted is a suspiciously secular-looking model of religion. If this model cannot handle the anthropological, historical, and other nontheological data better than do the alternatives, there is no reason to ask whether it can be religiously useful.

We shall look particularly at the problem of whether it is conceptually and empirically better to picture religions in expressivist fashion as products of those deep experiences of the divine (or the self, or the world) which most of us are accustomed to thinking of as peculiarly religious, or whether one should opt for the converse thesis that religions are producers of experience. It is important, however, to remember that this is not the only angle from which religions can be studied. They have many aspects: not only the cognitive, aesthetic (cf. experiential-expressive), and cultural-linguistic ones that chiefly concern us but also legal, moral, ritual, institutional, and psychological ones. Each of these dimensions can be a source of models in terms of which one seeks to organize one's understanding of all aspects of religion for particular purposes. All that is claimed in this chapter is that a cultural-linguistic approach is preferable to traditional cognitivist and experiential-expressive approaches, provided the aim is to give a nontheological account of the relations of religion and experience.

The argument consists chiefly of an extended comparison of experiential-expressive and cultural-linguistic approaches. I try to show that the cultural-linguistic alternative is intellectually and empirically the most adequate.

This approach avoids certain conceptual pitfalls and accounts for a wider range of aspects of religion than do either of the others.

As has already been indicated in the previous chapter, experiential-expressivism is so pervasive in contemporary theology and at the same time so variegated that it is hard to decide on any one author to serve as an instance. I have settled on Bernard Lonergan both because in this area he is engagingly succinct and because his two-dimensional approach takes account of a range of theological considerations, not least Roman Catholic ones, which will engage our attention in later chapters when we ask about the ecumenical availability of the proposals in this book.

On the cultural-linguistic side, the problem is that the nontheologians who have developed the approach have not, for reasons already indicated, been concerned about the theological uses of the model and have therefore not structured their presentations in ways that fit the aims of this book. I have therefore developed my own sketch, although out of largely borrowed elements.

I
AN EXPERIENTIAL-EXPRESSIVE MODEL

Four, and to some extent five, of the six theses in which Lonergan summarizes his theory of religion[1] are characteristic of experiential-expressivism in general: (1) Different religions are diverse expressions or objectifications of a common core experience. It is this experience which identifies them as religions. (2) The experience, while conscious, may be unknown on the level of self-conscious reflection. (3) It is present in all human beings. (4) In most religions, the experience is the source and norm of objectifications: it is by reference to the experience that their adequacy or lack of adequacy is to be judged.

A fifth point (which is fourth in Lonergan's original enumeration) characterizes the primordial religious experience as "God's gift of love"[2] or, when fully present, as "the dynamic state of being in love without restrictions" and "without an object."[3] This experience can also be designated in other ways: "Inasmuch as it is conscious without being known, the gift of God's love is an experience of the holy, of Rudolf Otto's *mysterium fascinans et tremendum*. It is what Paul Tillich named a being grasped by ultimate concern. It is what corresponds to Ignatius Loyola's consolation that has no cause, as expounded by Karl Rahner."[4] In this thesis, Lonergan is obviously speaking as a Christian theologian rather than simply as a theorist of religion. The same is true in a sixth thesis, according to which the objectivities of at least biblical religions are not simply the expressive symbolizations of experience but have also another source in God's revelatory will, which ensures that they constitute the proper and normative correlate of the experience. We shall have more to say about this, the theologically most interesting aspect of the theory, in the next chapter.

At present we need simply note that Lonergan assumes, as do most experiential-expressivist theologians, that the scholarly study of religious phenomena on the whole supports the crucial affirmation of the basic unity of religious experience. He grants, to be sure, that religious experience "varies with every difference of culture, class or individual"[5] and says, "There is, I suppose, no clear cut evidence to show that . . . religious experience conforms to the model I have set forth."[6] Nevertheless he takes for granted that the model accommodates the evidence better than does any other and cites Friedrich Heiler to that effect in a passage to which we shall later return.

Lonergan also has theological reasons (which will concern us later) for affirming the underlying unity of religious experience, but when looked at nontheologically, this is the most problematic element in his, as in other, experiential-expressive theories. Because this core experience is said to be common to a wide diversity of religions, it is difficult or impossible to specify its distinctive features, and yet unless this is done, the assertion of commonality becomes logically and empirically vacuous. Lonergan himself acknowledges that it is logically odd. He speaks of it as an experience of love, but also admits that it alone among inner, nonsensory experiences seems to be prior to all conceptualization or cognition. As many authors put it, it precedes the distinction between subject and object, or, in the words of Karl Rahner, it is the experience "in which what is meant and the experience of what is meant are still one."[7] These characterizations create a nest of problems that, as we shall now see, cultural-linguistic approaches avoid.

II

A CULTURAL-LINGUISTIC ALTERNATIVE

The description of the cultural-linguistic alternative that I shall now sketch is shaped by the ultimately theological concerns of the present inquiry, but it is consonant, I believe, with the anthropological, sociological, and philosophical studies by which it has been for the most part inspired. In the account that I shall give, religions are seen as comprehensive interpretive schemes, usually embodied in myths or narratives and heavily ritualized, which structure human experience and understanding of self and world. Not every telling of one of these cosmic stories is religious, however. It must be told with a particular purpose or interest. It must be used, to adopt a suggestion of William Christian, with a view to identifying and describing what is taken to be "more important than everything else in the universe,"[8] and to organizing all of life, including both behavior and beliefs, in relation to this. If the interpretive scheme is used or the story is told without this interest in the maximally important, it ceases to function religiously. To be sure, it may continue to shape in various ways the attitudes, sentiments, and conduct of individuals and of groups. A religion, in other words, may continue to exercise immense influence on the way people experience themselves and their world even when it is no longer explicitly adhered to.

Stated more technically, a religion can be viewed as a kind of cultural and/or linguistic framework or medium that shapes the entirety of life and thought. It functions somewhat like a Kantian *a priori,* although in this case the *a priori* is a set of acquired skills that could be different. It is not primarily an array of beliefs about the true and the good (though it may involve these), or a symbolism expressive of basic attitudes, feelings, or sentiments (though these will be generated). Rather, it is similar to an idiom that makes possible the description of realities, the formulation of beliefs, and the experiencing of inner attitudes, feelings, and sentiments. Like a culture or language, it is a communal phenomenon that shapes the subjectivities of individuals rather than being primarily a manifestation of those subjectivities. It comprises a vocabulary of discursive and nondiscursive symbols together with a distinctive logic or grammar in terms of which this vocabulary can be meaningfully deployed. Lastly, just as a language (or "language game," to use Wittgenstein's phrase) is correlated with a form of life, and just as a culture has both cognitive and behavioral dimensions, so it is also in the case of a religious tradition. Its doctrines, cosmic stories or myths, and ethical directives are integrally related to the rituals it practices, the sentiments or experiences it evokes, the actions it recommends, and the institutional forms it develops. All this is involved in comparing a religion to a cultural-linguistic system.

Turning now in more detail to the relation of religion and experience, it may be noted that this is not unilateral but dialectical. It is simplistic to say (as I earlier did) merely that religions produce experiences, for the causality is reciprocal. Patterns of experience alien to a given religion can profoundly influence it. The warrior passions of barbarian Teutons and Japanese occasioned great changes in originally pacifistic Christianity and Buddhism. These religions were pressed into service to sanction the values of militaristic societies and were largely transformed in the process. Yet in providing new legitimations for the ancient patterns, they also altered the latter. Presumably the inner experiences as well as the code of behavior of a Zen samurai or a Christian knight are markedly different from those of their pagan or pre-Buddhist predecessors. Yet, as this illustration shows, in the interplay between "inner" experience and "external" religious and cultural factors, the latter can be viewed as the leading partners, and it is this option which the cultural and/or linguistic analyst favors.

It remains true, therefore, that the most easily pictured of the contrasts between a linguistic-cultural model of religion and an experiential-expressive one is that the former reverses the relation of the inner and the outer. Instead of deriving external features of a religion from inner experience, it is the inner experiences which are viewed as derivative.

Thus the linguistic-cultural model is part of an outlook that stresses the degree to which human experience is shaped, molded, and in a sense constituted by cultural and linguistic forms. There are numberless thoughts we cannot think, sentiments we cannot have, and realities we cannot perceive unless we learn to use the appropriate symbol systems. It seems, as the cases of Helen Keller and of supposed wolf children vividly illustrate, that unless we acquire language of some kind, we cannot actualize our specifically human capacities for thought, action, and feeling.[9] Similarly, so the argument goes, to become religious involves becoming skilled in the language, the symbol system of a given religion. To become a Christian involves learning the story of Israel and of Jesus well enough to interpret and experience oneself and one's world in its terms. A religion is above all an external word, a *verbum externum,* that molds and shapes the self and its world, rather than an expression or thematization of a preexisting self or of preconceptual experience. The *verbum internum* (traditionally equated by Christians with the action of the Holy Spirit) is also crucially important, but it would be understood in a theological use of the model as a capacity for hearing and accepting the true religion, the true external word, rather than (as experiential-expressivism would have it) as a common experience diversely articulated in different religions.[10]

As has already been mentioned, part of the strength of a cultural-linguistic outlook is that it can accommodate and combine the distinctive and often competing emphases of the other two approaches. Consider, for example, the insight, foreign to a cognitivist outlook, represented by Paul Tillich's experiential-expressive formula that "religion is the substance of culture, and culture the form of religion"[11]—i.e., religion in the sense of ultimate concern is the vitalizing source of all significant cultural achievements. The alternative here proposed does not deny this, but offers a more complex formulation that transposes the emphases. Religion, one might say, is that ultimate dimension of culture (because it has to do with whatever is taken as most important) which gives shape and intensity to the experiential matrix from which significant cultural achievements flow. The basic imagery in this formulation is closer to Aristotelian hylomorphism than to the idealisms of Schelling or Hegel, by whom Tillich was influenced. In both cases, "form" may be inseparable from experiential "matter," but in a hylomorphic model, form has priority because experience, like matter, exists only insofar as it is informed. In the idealist model, in contrast, experience of a certain kind (i.e., "Spirit" or *Geist*) has a prior reality that necessarily expresses and fulfills itself in objective cultural and religious forms. In both models the culture-forming power of religious experience can be acknowledged, although in one case the experience is derivative, in the other primordial.

In thus inverting the relation of the internal and external dimensions of religion, linguistic and cultural approaches resemble cognitivist theories for which external (i.e., propositionally statable) beliefs are primary, but without the intellectualism of the latter. A comprehensive scheme or story used to structure all dimensions of existence is not primarily a set of propositions to be believed, but is rather the medium in which one moves, a set of skills that one employs in living one's life. Its vocabulary of symbols and its syntax may be used for many purposes, only one of which is the formulation of statements about reality. Thus while a religion's truth claims are often of the utmost importance to it (as in the case of Christianity), it is, nevertheless, the conceptual vocabulary and the syntax or inner logic which determine the kinds of truth claims the religion can make. The cognitive aspect, while often important, is not primary.

This stress on the code, rather than the (e.g., propositionally) encoded, enables a cultural-linguistic approach to accommodate the experiential-expressive concern for the unreflective dimensions of human existence far better than is possible in a cognitivist outlook. Religion cannot be pictured in the cognitivist (and voluntarist) manner as primarily a matter of deliberately choosing to believe or follow explicitly known propositions or directives. Rather, to become religious—no less than to become culturally or linguistically competent—is to interiorize a set of skills by practice and training. One learns how to feel, act, and think in conformity with a religious tradition that is, in its inner structure, far richer and more subtle than can be explicitly articulated. The primary knowledge is not *about* the religion, nor *that* the religion teaches such and such, but rather *how* to be religious in such and such ways. Sometimes explicitly formulated statements of the beliefs or behavioral norms of a religion may be helpful in the learning process, but by no means always. Ritual, prayer, and example are normally much more important. Thus—insofar as the experiential-expressive contrast between experience and knowledge is comparable to that between "knowing how" and "knowing that"—cultural-linguistic models, no less than expressive ones, emphasize the experiential or existential side of religion, though in a different way.

As a result there is also room for the expressive aspects. The aesthetic and nondiscursively symbolic dimensions of a religion—for example, its poetry, music, art, and rituals—are not, as propositional cognitivism suggests, mere external decorations designed to make the hard core of explicitly statable beliefs and precepts more appealing to the masses. Rather, it is through these that the basic patterns of religion are interiorized, exhibited, and transmitted. The proclamation of the gospel, as a Christian would put it, may be first of all the telling of the story, but this gains power and meaning insofar as it is embodied in the total gestalt of community life and action.

Furthermore, interiorized skill, the skill of the saint, manifests itself in an ability to discriminate "intuitively" (nondiscursively) between authentic and inauthentic, and between effective and ineffective, objectifications of the religion. Having been inwardly formed by a given tradition—by, for example, "the mind of Christ" (I Cor. 2:16), as Paul puts it—the saint has what Thomas Aquinas calls "connatural knowledge"[12] and by what Newman calls "the illative sense"[13] in matters religious. This is quite different from the reflective and theoretical knowledge of the trained theologian, who employs publicly assessable rules and procedures in seeking to distinguish between the good and the bad, the true and the false. Rather, it is like the grammatical or rhetorical knowledge of a poet such as Homer, who could not enunciate a single rule in either discipline and yet was able to sense as could no one else what conformed or did not conform to the spirit, the unarticulated rules, of the Greek language. On this view, the way a religion functions once it is interiorized is much better described in expressivist than in cognitivist terms.

There is a sense, then, in which experience and expression are no less important in a cultural-linguistic model than in an experiential-expressive one. Nevertheless, the nature of experience and its relation to expression and communication are construed quite differently. This brings us to the conceptual formulation of the major contrast between the two models, which we earlier spoke of in a pictorial fashion as a "reversal of the relation between the inner and outer."

When one pictures inner experiences as prior to expression and communication, it is natural to think of them in their most basic and elemental form as also prior to conceptualization or symbolization. If, in contrast, expressive and communicative symbol systems, whether linguistic or nonlinguistic, are primary—then, while there are of course nonreflective experiences, there are no uninterpreted or unschematized ones. On this view, the means of communication and expression are a precondition, a kind of quasi-transcendental (i.e., culturally formed) *a priori* for the possibility of experience. We cannot identify, describe, or recognize experience qua experience without the use of signs and symbols. These are necessary even for what the depth psychologist speaks of as "unconscious" or "subconscious" experiences, or for what the phenomenologist describes as prereflective ones. In short, it is necessary to have the means for expressing an experience in order to have it, and the richer our expressive or linguistic system, the more subtle, varied, and differentiated can be our experience.

This is a complex thesis, and its full discussion lies beyond the scope of this essay. A crude illustration of what is involved may, however, be helpful. There are reported to be tribal languages that do not discriminate between, e.g., green and blue, and the members of these tribes are reported (erroneously, according to some observers)[14] to have difficulty recognizing the difference between the two colors. They are not color-blind. On the physiological level, their retinas and optic nerves respond differentially to light waves of varying lengths just as ours do, but they lack the verbal categories for experiencing these differences in stimuli. Or, in order to avoid cultural provincialism, one can put the case conversely: we lack the linguistic *a priori* for having the visual experiences that they have.

Whether or not this particular illustration is veridical, it does raise the question of whether language influences domains of human reality that are generally thought of, not simply as prelinguistic, but as preexperiential, e.g., sensory physiological processes to which we as subjects do not have privileged access but of which we can become aware only by external observation of ourselves or others. It seems clear that even the presensory or preperceptual selection and organization of stimuli is not entirely prelinguistic. The classification and categorial patterns embedded in a language, once it has been acquired, help organize the inexperienceably chaotic confusion that bombards our senses. One can even plausibly propose (as have both Noam Chomsky,[15] on theoretical linguistic grounds, and Clifford Geertz,[16] on anthropological-evolutionary ones) that human beings are so thoroughly programmed genetically for language use that apart from acquiring a language they cannot properly develop physiologically as other animals do, but remain peculiarly immature in their sensory and physical competence. Further, once they do learn a language, this shapes the preexperiential physical basis of their conscious experience and activity. Thus language, it seems, shapes domains of human existence and action that are preexperiential. This is one of the senses in which the human being is a psychosomatic unity.

But the position that language (or, more generally, some conceptual and/or symbolic interpretive scheme) is a condition for religious experience need not be based on these perhaps empirically falsifiable speculations. It does not depend, in other words, on the possibility just mentioned that public linguistic categories shape even preexperiential activity. One could also claim that an experience (viz., something of which one is prereflectively or reflectively conscious) is impossible unless it is in some fashion symbolized, and that all symbol systems have their origin in interpersonal relations and social interactions. It is conceptually confused to talk of symbolizations (and therefore of experiences) that are purely private.

There are several ways of arguing this. The most ambitious is Wittgenstein's contention that private languages are logically impossible.[17] If so, the same would have to be said regarding private religious experiences (such as the dynamic state of being unrestrictedly in love), which are purportedly independent of any particular language game. This is not the place to assess this argument. I shall simply note that even those experiential-expressivists —such as Lonergan (or Karl Rahner and David Tracy)—who acknowledge that experience cannot be expressed except in public and intersubjective forms, do seem to maintain a kind of privacy in the origins of experience and language that, if Wittgenstein is right, is more than doubtful.[18]

A more modest argument does not try to demonstrate the impossibility of unthematized yet conscious experience but simply employs Ockham's razor to conclude that there is no need for this hypothesis. One way to make this point is by means of the classic medieval distinction between first and second intentions. As applied to objects *(intentio objectiva),* "animal" in the first intention is this or that creature, Fido or Socrates, in its own actual or possible, imaginary or real being, while in the second intention it is a generic concept embracing many species such as the human and the canine. As applied to mental activities *(intentio formalis),* the first intention is the act whereby we grasp objects, while the second intention is the reflex act of grasping or reflecting on first formal intentions. In the modern philosophical language of consciousness, we are only unthematically (or, in Polanyi's terminology, "tacitly")[19] aware of first intentional activities while we are engaged in them: our attention is focused on objects, not on the subjective experience involved in knowing them. It is only in the second intention that we attend to this experience, that we are focally rather than tacitly aware of it. Yet this does not lead us to suppose that the first-intentional experiences of, for example, attending to Fido or to the logical characteristics of the concept of animal are somehow preverbal or linguistically unstructured. Surely, so the argument goes, the same could be said of religious experiences. They can be construed as by-products of linguistically or conceptually structured cognitive activities of which we are not directly aware because they are first-intentional. The sense of the holy of which Rudolf Otto speaks can be construed as the tacit or unthematic awareness of applying a culturally acquired concept of the holy in a given situation. Similarly, concert pianists tell us that it is disastrous for them to become focally conscious of their fingers while they are playing, but nevertheless their playing (and their sometimes ecstatic experience of playing) depends on their fingering. It seems that the most economical hypothesis is to suppose that the relation between religious experiences and a given culture, language, and form of life is similar. If my application of the notions of first and second intentions is correct, then this is a thesis on which Thomas Aquinas and other medieval Aristotelians (but not all medieval Augustinians)[20] agree with Wittgenstein against post-Cartesian philosophers of consciousness as well as against some professed Thomists such as Lonergan and Rahner. For the Aristotelians, affective experiences (in which would be included a sense of the holy or of absolute dependence) always depend on prior cognition of objects, and the objects available to us in this life are all in some fashion constructed out of (or, in medieval terminology, "abstracted from") conceptually or linguistically structured sense experience.

Many modifications of common ways of thinking about religion follow from abandoning the notion that its source is in prior experience, but I shall mention only two. First, religious change or innovation must be understood, not as proceeding from new experiences, but as resulting from the interactions of a cultural-linguistic system with changing situations. Religious traditions are not transformed, abandoned, or replaced because of an upwelling of new or different ways of feeling about the self, world, or God, but because a religious interpretive scheme (embodied, as it always is, in religious practice and belief) develops anomalies in its application in new contexts. This produces, among other things, negative effects, negative experiences, even by the religion's own norms. Prophetic figures apprehend, often with dramatic vividness, how the inherited patterns of belief, practice, and ritual need to be (and can be) reminted. They discover the concepts that remove the anomalies. Religious experiences in the sense of feelings, sentiments, or emotions then result from the new conceptual patterns instead of being their source.

Thus, if one follows this account, Luther did not invent his doctrine of justification by faith because he had a tower experience,[21] but rather the tower experience was made possible by his discovering (or thinking he discovered) the doctrine in the Bible. To be sure, the experience of justification by faith occasioned by his exegesis then generated a variety of fresh expressive symbolisms, among which Lutherans like especially to mention the music of Johann Sebastian Bach. Without such powerful experiences and their effective expression, the tradition would have neither started nor persisted, yet logically, even if not causally, a religious experience and its expression are secondary and tertiary in a linguistic-cultural model. First come the objectivities of the religion, its language, doctrines, liturgies, and modes of action, and it is through these that passions are shaped into various kinds of what is called religious experience.

A second consequence of this outlook which is particularly important for our immediate purposes is that it raises questions regarding the meaningfulness of the notion that there is an inner experience of God common to all human beings and all religions. There can be no experiential core because, so the argument goes, the experiences that religions evoke and mold are as varied as the interpretive schemes they embody. Adherents of different religions do not diversely thematize the same experience; rather they have different experiences. Buddhist compassion, Christian love and—if I may cite a quasi-religious phenomenon—French Revolutionary *fraternité* are not diverse modifications of a single fundamental human awareness, emotion, attitude, or sentiment, but are radically (i.e., from the root) distinct ways of experiencing and being oriented toward self, neighbor, and cosmos. The affective features they have in common are part, so to speak, of their raw materials, functions of those feelings of closeness to one's immediate fellows shared by all human beings including Nazis and headhunters. Similarly, the sense of the holy or the sacred that is the identifying mark of religion for much of the experiential-expressive tradition is not a common quality, but a set of family resemblances. There may be some religions in which it is of little or no importance; and even those which emphasize it need not for that reason be similar. It may be as much a mistake to classify them together as to claim that all red things, whether apples, Indians, or the Moscow square belong to the same natural genus. Much the same can be said regarding mystical experiences. What these have in common can be easily understood quite naturalistically as consisting, for example, of the "oceanic feelings" of which Freud spoke.[22] To be sure, in a cultural-linguistic outlook one would add (as Freud did not) that these feelings become ingredients in a wide variety of experiences of the world, of self, and—the believer would say—of God that depend on different perceptual categories (e.g., religious or nonreligious, theistic or nontheistic) and forms of practice (e.g., drug-taking, yoga exercises, contemplative prayer).[23] Thus religion, including mysticism, need not be described as something universal arising from within the depths of individuals and diversely and inadequately objectified in particular faiths; it can at least as plausibly be construed as a class name for a variegated set of cultural-linguistic systems that, at least in some cases, differentially shape and produce our most profound sentiments, attitudes, and awarenesses.

In summary, the alternate model understands religions as idioms for dealing with whatever is most important—with ultimate questions of life and death, right and wrong, chaos and order, meaning and meaninglessness. These are the problems they treat in their stories, myths, and doctrines. They imprint their answers through rites, instruction, and other socializing processes, not only on the conscious mind but in the individual and cultural subconscious. Thus a Balinese, molded by a ceremonial system in which is embedded a partly Hindu and partly animist world view, will fall into a catatonic trance when confronted by types of stimulus that might plunge a Westerner, influenced by a long tradition of biblical monotheism, into strenuous activity.[24] Centuries of ritual reiteration of certain definitions of what is ultimately good and true have so shaped these two cultural types that their basic attitudinal reflexes are different even in the absence of belief or of much explicit knowledge of the religious traditions. In the face of such examples, it seems implausible to claim that religions are diverse objectifications of the same basic experience. On the contrary, different religions seem in many cases to produce fundamentally divergent depth experiences of what it is to be human. The empirically available data seem to support a cultural-linguistic rather than an experiential-expressive understanding of the relation of religion and experience.

III
THE INCONCLUSIVENESS OF THE COMPARISON

Yet it should not be thought that the decision between the theories we are comparing can be made on empirical grounds alone. We are confronted with all-embracing and fundamentally different notions of what religion is, and each of them shapes the view of what is relevant evidence for or against its own truth. This can be illustrated by reference to Friedrich Heiler, whom Lonergan cites at greater length than any other author, in favor of the view that the higher religions come from one and the same root experience of transcendence. Heiler claims that Christianity, Judaism, Islam, Zoroastrianism, Hinduism, Buddhism, and Taoism hold "that there is a transcendent reality; that he is immanent in human hearts; that he is supreme beauty, truth, righteousness, goodness; that he is love, mercy, compassion; that the way to him is repentance, self-denial, prayer; that the way is love of one's neighbor, even of one's enemies; that the way is love of God, union with him, or dissolution into him."[25] Heiler is a learned man, and he makes a plausible case that if one wants to find similarities in the world's major religions, *and* if one looks at them through Christian eyes, then this is a defensible list of the elements they have in common. It seems certain, however, that an adherent of an Eastern religion embarked on a similar task would formulate a very different list that would make Christianity sound rather like Taoism or Buddhism, for example, rather than vice versa.

This is one reason cultural-linguistic theorists are unimpressed by efforts to show that all religions are basically similar, but there is also another reason. One does not establish that two languages are alike, so they might argue, by showing that both use overlapping sets of sounds or have common objects of reference (e.g., mother, child, water, fire, and all the more salient persons and objects in the world human beings share). What counts in determining similarities between languages are the grammatical patterns, the ways of referring, the semantic and syntactic structures. Something at least remotely analogous can be said to hold in the case of religions. The datum that all religions recommend something which can be called "love" toward that which is taken to be most important ("God") is a banality as uninteresting as the fact that all languages are (or were) spoken. The significant things are the distinctive patterns of story, belief, ritual, and behavior that give "love" and "God" their specific and sometimes contradictory meanings.

Yet devastating though this rejoinder may seem to those unsympathetic with experiential-expressive theories, it is not conclusive. At most it shows that an experiential-expressivist position is unprovable, but does not demonstrate that it is false. It remains possible that, just as much the same emotions of (for example) joy or sorrow can be symbolically expressed or evoked by stories about different people or paintings of different style and subject matter, so also with the depth experiences of religion. The issues involved in this debate are even less susceptible to clear-cut decision than are comparable questions about the best overall theories in the physical sciences; and these, if T. S. Kuhn and others are to be believed, are never finally decidable. Theories are abandoned, not so much because they are refuted (on their own terms, that is), but because they prove unfruitful for new or different questions that come to interest the relevant group of scientists for a wide variety of reasons. The old theories may still hold perfectly well in their primary areas of application: mechanics, for example, remains to this day entirely Newtonian, untouched by Einstein's theory of relativity. Similarly, the inferiority of experiential-expressivism for the scientific study of religion may be quite compatible with its superiority for other purposes (for example, theological ones). Whether this is in fact the case is the question to which we now turn.

NOTES

1. Bernard Lonergan, *Method in Theology* (Herder & Herder, 1972), pp. 101–124.

2. Ibid., p. 105.

3. Ibid., pp. 120, 122.

4. Ibid., p. 106.

5. Bernard Lonergan, *Philosophy of God, and Theology* (London: Darton, Longman & Todd, 1973), p. 50.

6. Lonergan, *Method in Theology*, p. 108. To be sure, as we shall see in the next chapter, Lonergan holds that there are theological reasons for accepting the model.

7. Karl Rahner, *Foundations of Christian Faith* (Seabury Press, 1978), p. 17.

8. William A. Christian, Sr., *Meaning and Truth in Religion* (Princeton University Press, 1964), pp. 60ff. The question of how exactly to define religion is not important for the contrast between the two approaches that we are comparing, provided one insists, as Christian does, that the predicate (e.g., "most important") names a function rather than either a feeling or an experience, on the one hand, or an attribute or a character of the religious object, on the other. The reason for this stipulation is that there appears to be no common experience or attribute that applies within all the things that are normally called religions. David Little and Sumner B. Twiss, *Comparative Religious Ethics* (Harper & Row, 1978), seek to improve on Christian's definition of religion (p. 56), but their proposal has the disadvantage of doing violence to ordinary usage by giving a functional rather than an experiential or attributive meaning to "sacred" (pp. 59–60).

9. Susanne Langer, *Philosophy in a New Key* (Pelican Books, 1948), pp. 50-51, 83ff.

10. The priority of the *verbum externum* was a major emphasis of the Protestant Reformers against the spiritualists of the sixteenth century, but it was also part of the pre-Reformation tradition. Aquinas, for example, insisted that saving faith comes *ex auditu* (Rom. 10:17). Thus, contrary to some modern interpreters such as Rahner, the notion of "implicit faith" did not for him refer to the *verbum internum* (i.e., an unthematized, preconceptual experience of the divine), but rather presupposed some degree of explicit faith in the *verbum externum*. See Joseph DiNoia, "Implicit Faith, General Revelation and the State of Non-Christians," *The Thomist* 47/2 (1983), pp. 209–241. Cf. George Lindbeck, *"Fides ex Auditu* and the Salvation of Non-Christians: Contemporary Catholic and Protestant Positions," ed. by V. Vajta, *The Gospel and the Ambiguity of the Church* (Fortress Press, 1974), pp. 91–123.

11. Paul Tillich, *Systematic Theology,* Vol. 3 (University of Chicago Press, 1963), pp. 248ff. This is the last of many treatments of the theme by Tillich.

12. Thomas Aquinas, *ST* II-II.45.2; cf. I.1.6, ad 3.

13. John Henry Newman, *An Essay in Aid of a Grammar of Assent* (London, 1870).

14. B. Berlin and P. Kay, *Basic Color Terms* (University of California Press, 1969). Cf. M. Sahlins, "Colors and Cultures," *Semiotica* 16 (1976), pp. 1–22.

15. Noam Chomsky, *Language and Mind,* extended ed. (Harcourt Brace Jovanovich, 1972).

16. Clifford Geertz, "The Growth of Culture and the Evolution of Mind," *The Interpretation of Cultures* (Basic Books, 1973), pp. 55–86.

17. For a comprehensive exposition of Wittgenstein's scattered references see Robert J. Fogelin, *Wittgenstein* (London: Routledge & Kegan Paul, 1980), pp. 153–171.

18. Karl Rahner affirms an experience of the *"Vorgriff auf esse"* which is distinguishable, though not separable, from its categorial, conceptual, or linguistic schematization and is the transcendental condition of all human knowing and willing. See his *Spirit in the World,* tr. by William Dych (Herder & Herder, 1968), pp.

132–236. Cf. George Lindbeck, "The *A Priori* in St. Thomas' Theory of Knowledge," in Robert E. Cushman and Egil Grislis (eds.), *The Heritage of Christian Thought* (Harper & Row, 1965), pp. 41–63, for an evaluation of Rahner's argument that his position is in agreement with that of Aquinas.

David Tracy's position is structurally similar, although, unlike Rahner, the details of his argument are influenced more by Lonergan than by Marechal. He speaks of the "common human experience" of basic confidence or trust which grounds our commitments to the ultimate meaningfulness or worth of inquiring, deciding, and doing. Religious language and symbols more or less adequately "re-present" and reaffirm this basic experience on the level of self-conscious belief. See *Blessed Rage for Order: The New Pluralism in Theology* (Seabury Press, 1975), esp. pp. 97–103.

Lonergan, unlike Rahner and Tracy, does not speak of an "experience" of the transcendental conditions for human knowing and willing (inquiry, reflection, and deliberation), nor of religion as the symbolization of "common human experience," but rather of the special religious experience of the gift of God's love (and this is postulated on the basis of theological rather than philosophical considerations). Thus, unlike Tracy and Rahner, he seems to have only theological reasons for rejecting the thesis of the present book that intersubjective communicative systems are the source rather than the product of distinctively human experience, whether religious or nonreligious.

In view of Lonergan's attack on what he takes to be Wittgenstein's views on private language (*Method in Theology,* pp. 254–256), it might be thought that he is committed to prelinguistic experience, but the attack, if I understand it rightly, is based on the misapprehension that a denial of private languages entails a denial of mental acts. According to Peter Geach, *Mental Acts: Their Content and Their Objects* (London: Routledge & Kegan Paul, 1971), Gilbert Ryle makes the converse mistake: he thinks the affirmation of mental acts entails the affirmation of private languages; Aquinas, in contrast, denies private languages yet affirms mental acts (pp. 130–131). If so, the private language argument against prelinguistic experiences would be fully acceptable to Aquinas, but not to Tracy or Rahner, and, to a lesser extent, not to Lonergan.

The crucial philosophical issue is the validity of transcendental deductions of the necessary conditions of human knowing and willing. If the postulation of such conditions by means of transcendental arguments is valid, then it makes sense to say that one may experience these (e.g., the *Vorgriff auf esse*) prior to, even if not separable from, their thematization by linguistic or other conceptual systems. For a succinct statement of what, as far as I know, is an unanswered objection to transcendental deductions, see Stephan Körner, *Fundamental Questions in Philosophy* (Penguin Books, University Books, 1971), pp. 213ff.

19. The idea of using Polanyi's terminology to say that what is tacit in the first intention becomes focal in the second came to me while reading Robert E. McInnis, "Meaning, Thought and Language in Polanyi's Epistemology," *Philosophy Today* (Spring 1974), pp. 47–67, and "Polanyi's Model of Mental Acts," *The New Scholasticism* 47/2 (1973), pp. 147–180. Neither Polanyi nor McInnis draws the parallel, however.

20. Cf. my article cited in n. 18, above.

21. Assuming that it occurred. This illustration serves, no matter what the truth regarding the much-debated tower experience. What is important for our purposes is the contention that the core of Luther's reformatory breakthrough was an exegetical insight. See George Lindbeck, "Erikson's *Young Man Luther*: A Historical and Theological Reappraisal," *Soundings* 16 (1973), pp. 210–227, reprinted in Donald Capps et al. (eds.), *Encounter with Erikson* (Scholars Press, 1977), pp. 7–28.

22. Sigmund Freud, *Civilization and Its Discontents* (W. W. Norton & Co., 1961), pp. 11–20.

23. On the varieties of mystical experience see R. C. Zaehner, *Mysticism, Sacred and Profane* (Oxford: Clarendon Press, 1957), and Steven Katz, "Language Epistemology, and Mysticism," *Mysticism and Philosophical Analysis*, ed. by S. Katz (London: Sheldon Press, 1978), pp. 22–74.

24. The Balinese reference is to the Rangda-Barong temple dramas, of which one can find a brief description in Geertz, "The Growth of Culture and the Evolution of Mind," in his *The Interpretation of Cultures,* pp. 18Of. Cf. his essay on "The Impact of the Concept of Culture on the Science of Man," ibid., pp. 33–55.

25. Lonergan, *Method in Theology,* p. 109. This quotation is Lonergan's summary of Friedrich Heiler, "The History of Religion as a Preparation for the Cooperation of Religions," in Mircea Eliade and Joseph Kitagawa (eds.), *The History of Religions* (University of Chicago Press, 1959), pp. 142–153.

CHAPTER 3

MANY RELIGIONS
AND THE ONE TRUE FAITH

It is not the business of a nontheological theory of religion to argue for or against the superiority of any one faith, but it does have the job, if it is to be religiously useful, of allowing the possibility of such a superiority. It must not, in other words, exclude the claims religions make about themselves, and it must supply some interpretation of what these claims mean. If it cannot do this, it is at most of interest to purely scholarly students of religion and cannot be used by theologians and others who are religiously concerned.

It may be, as has already been noted, that one of the reasons for the theological neglect of cultural-linguistic approaches is that at first glance they do not seem well suited to meet these requirements. One language or culture is not generally thought of as "truer" than another, much less unsurpassable, and yet that is what some religions profess to be. The claim to finality is widespread in Western (or, more precisely, Middle Eastern) monotheisms, whether Jewish, Christian, or Islamic, and it appears to be at least implicit in Buddhism and some forms of Hinduism insofar as these function as nontribal, i.e., universal, religions. Can the possible truth of one or another of these assertions of unsurpassability be admitted; or, more precisely, what could such an assertion mean? Could it be interpreted in such a way as to allow for the desirability of nonproselytizing interreligious dialogue and cooperation, and for the possibility of salvation, however defined, outside the one true faith, if there is such a thing? We have already noted that nonproselytizing interreligious dialogue and the salvation of nonbelievers is of great importance to many people in our day. Indeed, both have been officially affirmed by the largest of all organized religious bodies, the Roman Catholic Church, at Vatican II.[1] If a cultural-linguistic approach cannot make at least as good sense of these emphases as do alternative theories of religion, then it will be rightly regarded as theologically uninteresting.

These interreligious problems—unsurpassability, dialogue, and the salvation of "other-believers"—are dealt with in the first three sections of the present chapter and are followed by a somewhat technical excursus on the notion of "truth" in a cultural-linguistic context. The next two chapters continue the discussion of theological issues, but in reference to the intrareligious rather than interreligious problems of doctrinal diversity and teaching authority within the single religion of Christianity. The agenda, it will be noted, is shaped by Christian concerns: a different selection of topics would have been made by, for example, a Buddhist or a Muslim. Yet despite this focus on the specifically Christian availability of a cultural-linguistic approach, it is possible that much of what is said also has applications to other religions.

I
UNSURPASSABILITY

Depending on the model that one uses, religions can be compared with each other in terms of their propositional truth, their symbolic efficacy, or their categorial adequacy. It will be useful to look at each of these terms separately before we turn to the differing notions of unsurpassability that they involve.

Those who are to some degree traditionally orthodox understand the propositional truth that they attribute to religious statements as a function of the ontological correspondence or "isomorphism" of the "structure of knowing and the structure of the known."[2] Each proposition or act of judgment corresponds or does not correspond, is eternally true or false: there are no degrees or variations in propositional truth. Nevertheless, a religion may be a mixture of true and false statements, and the primary question when comparing religions in the classically cognitivist approach of traditional orthodoxy is the question as to which faith makes the most significant veridical truth claims and the fewest false ones.

In an experiential-expressivist approach, in contrast, "truth" is a function of symbolic efficacy. Religions are most likely to be compared, if at all, in terms of how effectively they articulate or represent and communicate that inner experience of the divine (or, perhaps, of the "unconditioned") which is held to be common to them all. All religions are by definition capable of functioning truly in this nondiscursive, symbolic sense, but they can vary in their potential or actual degree of truth (i.e., efficacy).

Lastly, in a cultural-linguistic outlook, religions are thought of primarily as different idioms for construing reality, expressing experience, and ordering life. Attention, when considering the question of truth, focuses on the categories (or "grammar," or "rules of the game") in terms of which truth claims are made and expressive symbolisms employed. Thus the questions raised in comparing religions have to do first of all with the adequacy of their categories. Adequate categories are those which can be made to apply to what is taken to be real, and which therefore make possible, though they do not guarantee, propositional, practical, and symbolic truth. A religion that is thought of as having such categories can be said to be "categorially true."

There is a certain novelty in applying notions of categorial adequacy or truth to religions, and some illustrations are therefore in order. Religions may be compared to mathematical systems, for example, because these latter are not by themselves propositionally true or false in the ontological sense, but rather constitute the only idioms in which first-order (or first-intentional) truths and falsehoods can be stated regarding the quantifiable aspects of reality. It is, for example, meaningless to say that one thing is larger than another if one lacks the categorial concept of size. Yet their categorial adequacy does not guarantee propositional truth, but only makes meaningful statements possible: if something is quantifiable, statements about its size have meaning, but not necessarily truth. Similarly a categorially true religion would be one in which it is possible to speak meaningfully of that which is, e.g., most important; but meaningfulness, it should be remembered, makes possible propositional falsehood as well as truth.

Secondly, the difference between religions may in some cases be analogous to that between mathematical and nonmathematical—e.g., quantitative and qualitative—descriptions of reality. They may, in other words, be incommensurable in such a way that no equivalents can be found in one language or religion for the crucial terms of the other. "Larger" cannot be translated by "redder," for example, because that would result in descriptive nonsense: e.g., the red flag is larger than the Red Square in Moscow because it is redder, and vice versa. Similarly, the means for referring in any direct way to the Buddhist Nirvana are lacking in Western religions and the cultures influenced by them and it is, therefore, at least initially puzzling how one can say anything either true or false about Nirvana, or even meaningfully deny it, within these latter contexts. Or, to push the same point farther, many Christians have maintained that the stories about Abraham, Isaac, Jacob, and Jesus are part of the referential meaning of the word "God" as this is used in biblical religion and have therefore concluded that philosophers and others who do not advert to these narratives mean something else by "God."[3] The God of the philosophers may or may not exist and may or may not in some respects be assimilable to the God of the Bible, but faith in the biblical deity, according to this view, is logically independent of philosophical arguments over these questions.

In short, the cultural-linguistic approach is open to the possibility that different religions and/or philosophies may have incommensurable notions of truth, of experience, and of categorial adequacy, and therefore also of what it would mean for something to be most important (i.e., "God"). Unlike other perspectives, this approach proposes no common framework such as that supplied by the propositionalist's concept of truth or the expressivist's concept of experience within which to compare religions. Thus when affirmations or ideas from categorially different religious or philosophical frameworks are introduced into a given religious outlook, these are either simply babbling or else, like mathematical formulas employed in a poetic text, they have vastly different functions and meanings than they had in their original settings.

The three senses of "true" that we have distinguished yield three contrasting interpretations of the claim that a given religion is unsurpassable. The traditionally most familiar version of this claim is the propositional one. According to this, the final religion must be exempt from error (for otherwise it could be surpassed). This propositional inerrancy has usually been attributed in Christianity to the original "deposit of faith," though it has also been ascribed to Scripture and *de fide* church doctrines. Another logically necessary requirement is that the unsurpassable religion contain the highest of what Aquinas called *revelabilia* (i.e., religiously significant truths capable of being revealed within the space-time world of human experience).[4] It might otherwise be entirely yet incompletely true and therefore surpassable. Such has been one traditional Christian attitude toward the religion of Israel. Properly understood, Old Testament religion contains no falsehoods, yet higher truths can be (and indeed have been) revealed. Most religions, however, are thought of as a mixture of truth and error. Yet it is not logically impossible, though it is traditionally not emphasized,[5] that partly false religions may contain truths of an important though subordinate nature that are not initially present in the highest religion and can therefore enrich it.

When religions are thought of as expressively rather than propositionally true, this possibility of complementarity and mutual enrichment is increased, but it also becomes hard to attach any definite meaning to the notion of "unsurpassably true." Mutual enrichment increases because, as we noted earlier, the various religions are seen as objectifications of the same basic experiences and can possibly teach each other more, not only about peripheral matters but also about their common core. The difficulty of specifying a meaning for "unsurpassably true" in an experiential-expressive framework is similar to the problem of identifying a referent for "unsurpassably evocative of aesthetic pleasure" or, less aptly, "unsurpassably strongest" or "unsurpassably reddest." The point of these comparisons is that when truth is understood in terms of symbolic efficacy it is a variable quality without any logically intrinsic upper limit (though it may have a de facto one). It is always possible conceptually, even if not physically, to project an intenser red, or greater strength, or more supernal beauty, or more adequate and effective symbolism. Secondly, there is no intrinsic reason why there should not be many equal but distinct instances of the highest actual degree of any of these qualities, including symbolic power.

To be sure, expressive truth can be unsurpassable, but only in a weak sense. If there is in existence a religion that is in fact highest, and if human history terminates before it is excelled, then it will become not only unsurpassed, but unsurpassable. This is a purely eschatological finality in the sense of having to do with the end of time as we know it, and is thus, so to speak, a mere historical accident. Maurice Wiles argues in expressivist fashion that this was the only kind of finality that the early Christians attributed to Christianity: they anticipated no greater experience of the divine than that mediated through Jesus Christ because they believed that history was about to end. It follows from this, so Wiles suggests, that the quite different propositional or ontological unsurpassability affirmed of Christ by, for example, the Nicene *homoousion* ("consubstantial with the Father") was the illicit—or at least not now binding—product of the desire to maintain finality even after its original presupposition, the imminence of the Parousia, had disappeared.[6] Whether this expressivist interpretation is the best or most plausible way of understanding the unsurpassability asserted of Christianity by the Trinitarian and Christological developments of the first centuries is a question to which we shall return in the next chapter.

The categorial form of the claim to unsurpassable truth can be incomparably stronger than the expressive one, but it may also be, in different respects, both stronger and weaker than the propositional claim. It could be—to take the strongest version first—that there is only one religion which has the concepts and categories that enable it to refer to the religious object, i.e., to whatever in fact is more important than everything else in the universe. This religion would then be the only one in which any form of propositional, and conceivably also expressive, religious truth or falsity could be present. Other religions might then be called categorially false, but propositionally and expressively they would be neither true nor false. They would be religiously meaningless just as talk about light and heavy things is meaningless when one lacks the concept "weight." This is a more forceful claim to unsurpassable truth than any that can be mounted, not only in expressivist but also in propositional terms. When one thinks of religions in a cognitivist fashion they are always at least meaningful enough to be false, and the most diabolical can contain some glimmers of truth even if it be no more than the belief that there is a devil. On a categorial interpretation, in contrast, beliefs about the Satan of Satanism might be neither true nor false, but like those regarding a square circle, nonsensical (though horrendously so).

There is also, however, as we have said, a sense in which categorial unsurpassability and truth is weaker than the propositional variety. Categorial truth does not exclude propositional error. Rather, it makes error as well as truth possible. Even if there is only one religion in which reference to God can occur (if there is such a being) yet it will be open to all sorts of falsehoods in what it affirms of him. This sounds outrageous to traditionally pious ears. It is ordinarily thought that a religion must correspond in its propositions fully and faithfully to divine reality in order for it to be the only true one.

Part of the problem, perhaps, is that in a culture influenced by what Lonergan calls the systematic differentiation of consciousness,[7] even ordinary common sense supposes that truth by correspondence must be propositional. Both the Protestant who insists on scriptural inerrancy and the Roman Catholic traditionalist counterpart are likely to be suffering from vulgarized forms of a rationalism descended from Greek philosophy by way of Cartesian and post-Cartesian rationalism reinforced by Newtonian science; but in the early centuries of the church, ontological truth by correspondence had not yet been limited to propositionalism. Fundamentalist literalism, like experiential-expressivism, is a product of modernity.

There is, these comments assume, a sense in which truth as correspondence can retain its significance even for a religion whose truth is primarily categorial rather than propositional. A religion thought of as comparable to a cultural system, as a set of language games correlated with a form of life, may as a whole correspond or not correspond to what a theist calls God's being and will. As actually lived, a religion may be pictured as a single gigantic proposition. It is a true proposition to the extent that its objectivities are interiorized and exercised by groups and individuals in such a way as to conform them in some measure in the various dimensions of their existence to the ultimate reality and goodness that lies at the heart of things. It is a false proposition to the extent that this does not happen.

We shall return in more systematic fashion at the end of this chapter to the relation of categorial, propositional, and ontological truth, but first let us try a cartographic simile.[8] A map, let us stipulate, becomes a proposition, an affirmation about how to travel from one place to another, only when actually utilized in the course of a journey. To the extent that the map is misread and misused, it is a part of a false proposition no matter how accurate it may be in itself. Conversely, even if it is in many ways in error in its distances, proportions, and topographic markings, it becomes constitutive of a true proposition when it guides the traveler rightly. A map of imaginary space, in contrast, cannot be used (because it is categorially false) to formulate ontologically true or false propositions, but only meaningless ones; while one of irrelevant space (e.g., of the South Pacific when the goal is Jerusalem) may truly correspond to reality but provides neither good nor bad guidance for the quest. Maps of the right space, in contrast, may become propositionally true or false. Some may be deliberately misleading, worse than irrelevant maps, not because they omit Jerusalem, but because they positively recommend against it, sending the traveler instead, e.g., to New York or Moscow. Others may be capable of becoming true, although varying greatly in completeness and accuracy. Some may initially point the pilgrim in the right general direction but become disconcertingly vague the farther one progresses as to where Jerusalem is located. Finally, there are the various versions of the final, complete, unsurpassable map that with varying degrees of detail and accuracy sufficiently identify the goal and the way (when they are rightly utilized) to enable the traveler not to go astray. Some of these versions may be mere sketches containing many inaccurate details, while others may be masterpieces of the cartographer's art, but the crucial factor at both extremes is how they are used. An inaccurate sketch may suffice to guide correctly those who are conscientious and skillful, while a cartographic masterpiece may be employed by perverse and careless vagabonds to justify taking whatever road seems most appealing even if it leads west rather than east, or north rather than south. Similarly, to draw the moral of the metaphor, the categorially and unsurpassably true religion is capable of being rightly utilized, of guiding thought, passions, and action in a way that corresponds to ultimate reality, and of thus being ontologically (and "propositionally") true, but is not always and perhaps not even usually so employed.

II
THE INTERRELATIONSHIPS OF RELIGIONS

After this allegorical account of the diversity of religions, it will be well to enumerate their possible relations in more prosaic fashion before turning to the implications for interreligious dialogue. First, there is the relation of the incomplete to the complete, of promise to fulfillment. Whatever one thinks of Christianity's traditional claim that it is thus related to Judaism, or of Islam's claim to be related in a somewhat similar way to both Judaism and Christianity, it is at least a logically possible relation. Second, some aspects of some religions, as the experiential-expressive model suggests, may diversely objectify the same or similar experiences. Meister Eckhart's and

Shankara's descriptions of mystical union, for example, seem to refer to the same experiential reality, yet one places this on the road to Jerusalem, and the other in a Vedanta Hindu map of the cosmos. As a consequence, the implications for praxis are notably different, and there is reason to suspect, especially if one takes a cultural-linguistic view, that the mystical experiences themselves diverge more than their descriptions indicate.[9] Third, religions may be complementary in the sense that they provide guidance to different but not incompatible dimensions of existence. Perhaps, for example, Buddhists know more about contemplation, and Christians about social action, and perhaps they can learn from each other in these domains even while retaining their categorially different notions of the maximally important. Fourth, however, direct opposition is also possible. Religions may give contrary directions, not only in the sense of charting different areas but by designating opposing goals and roads within common or overlapping maps of recognizably similar terrain. Such is the professed opposition of higher religions to Nazism, for example, or to Satanism (at least of the serious rather than the playacting variety). Fifth, there is the relation of the coherent to the incoherent or of the authentic to the inauthentic.[10] Some religions may provide maps that cannot be followed without inconsistency, affectation, or superficiality, and all religions, even the best, can spawn versions that systematically promote these diseases, not only in individuals but in groups. Thus authentic believers, whether Buddhist, Marxist, or biblical, may often be existentially and morally closer to each other than to many adherents of their own faiths. Their languages may be as different as Leibniz's calculus and Shakespeare's sonnets so that translation between them is impossible, and yet they may be united by the love they have for their respective tongues and the sensitivity and accuracy with which they use them. Finally, most religions are comparable in more than one of these respects. Depending on the aspect, they may be related to each other from their own perspectives as complete to incomplete, different expressions of similar experiences, complementary, opposed, and authentic or inauthentic; but, on the other hand, they may also be related in only one of these ways.

Given these interconnections, what is to be said of dialogue between religions? The desire to affirm dialogue, we recall, as well as the possibility of salvation for adherents of other religions (about which more in the next section) is a major cause for the popularity of experiential-expressive approaches. How can the cultural-linguistic alternative accommodate this desire?

The cultural-linguistic approach can allow a strong case for interreligious dialogue, but not for any single type of such dialogue. The currently favorite motive of cooperatively exploring common experiences is not entirely excluded, but it is not likely to dominate. The legitimate reasons for discussion are as varied as in international relations. Granted that a shrinking world makes it more and more imperative that religions no less than nations learn to communicate—but does it help in doing this to think that their deepest experiences and commitments must somehow be basically the same? Does not such a theory of dialogue run the danger of disguising the multiplicity of problems and motives?

However these questions are answered, there are other possible theological grounds for dialogue, varying from religion to religion, which do not presuppose that religions share an experiential core. For example, it can be argued in a variety of ways that Christian churches are called upon to imitate their Lord by selfless service to neighbors quite apart from the question of whether this promotes conversions. They also have scriptural authorization in such passages as Amos 9:7–8 for holding that nations other than Israel—and, by extension, religions other than the biblical ones—are also peoples elected (and failing) to carry out their own distinctive tasks within God's world. If so, not everything that pertains to the coming of the kingdom has been entrusted to that people of explicit witness which knows what and where Jerusalem is and (as believers hope) marches toward it, if only in fits and starts. It follows from these considerations that Christians may have a responsibility to help other movements and other religions make their own particular contributions, which may be quite distinct from the Christian one, to the preparation for the Consummation. The missionary task of Christians may at times be to encourage Marxists to become better Marxists, Jews and Muslims to become better Jews and Muslims, and Buddhists to become better Buddhists (although admittedly their notion of what a "better Marxist," etc., is will be influenced by Christian norms). Obviously this cannot be done without the most intensive and arduous conversation and cooperation.

It should not be thought that this is a novel suggestion. It is already in large part the official policy of major churches. The Declaration on Non-Christian Religions at the Second Vatican Council, for example, makes it quite clear that the purpose of dialogue need not be to convert, but may be rather to benefit other religions.[11] No fully developed theological rationale for this is presented by the Council, but the one we have outlined seems to have clear advantages in terms of the respect it accords other religions over an experiential-expressive type. One can admit the unsubstitutable uniqueness of the God-willed missions of non-Christian religions when one thinks of these faiths, not as objectifying poorly what Christianity objectifies well (as Karl Rahner proposes), but as cultural-linguistic systems within which potentialities can be actualized and realities explored that are not within the direct purview of the peoples of Messianic witness, but that are nevertheless

God-willed and God-approved anticipations of aspects of the coming kingdom.[12]

This obviously is a biblical argument for a practice of interreligious dialogue that was unthinkable in biblical times and that the Bible nowhere discusses, either to approve or disapprove. Because it draws on specifically biblical considerations, it cannot be proposed for adoption by nonbiblical religions. Because these are in their own right comprehensive cultural-linguistic systems, they must develop their own reasons, which may or may not include a desire, analogous to the one here suggested for Christians, for promoting the welfare of others. In other words, different religions are likely to have different warrants for interreligious conversation and cooperation. This lack of a common foundation is a weakness, but is also a strength. It means, on the one hand, that the partners in dialogue do not start with the conviction that they really basically agree, but it also means that they are not forced into the dilemma of thinking of themselves as representing a superior (or an inferior) articulation of a common experience of which the other religions are inferior (or superior) expressions. They can regard themselves as simply different and can proceed to explore their agreements and disagreements without necessarily engaging in the invidious comparisons that the assumption of a common experiential core make so tempting. In short, while a cultural-linguistic approach does not issue a blanket endorsement of the enthusiasm and warm fellow-feelings that can be easily promoted in an experiential-expressive context, it does not exclude the development of powerful theological rationales for sober and practically efficacious commitment to interreligious discussion and cooperation.

III
SALVATION AND OTHER FAITHS

What, however, of the salvation of those who belong to other religions or no religion at all? They would seem inevitably to have less of a chance than those who adhere to the one true faith. Or, to put it another way, there must be some value in being religiously right if this is to be preferred to being religiously wrong. Yet this conviction, indispensable though it is for religious self-respect, appears to imperil dialogue. If those who believe otherwise, whose map of the cosmos is different from one's own, are thereby hindered (or, worse, excluded) from salvation, then it would be inhumane to leave them to their fate rather than to seek by every possible means to convert them to the true Way. The claim of superiority or unsurpassability, when combined with concern for fellow human beings, would seem to lead almost inevitably to polemics and proselytizing instead of the dialogical and cooperative attitudes toward other religions favored officially (e.g., by Vatican II) or unofficially by a large proportion of contemporary religious people. We have postponed this question, but it is crucial for interreligious relations.

Each religion has its own way of formulating this problem—the role of Enlightenment and of Gautama's teachings for the Buddhist, of the Torah for the Jew, of the Koran and Muhammad for the Muslim—but in the Christian tradition, the question centers on salvation *solo Christo,* by Christ alone, and the major dilemma is how to reconcile this with the salvation of non-Christians. We are not here concerned with those who deny either the salvation of non-Christians (as do most Protestant and Catholic traditionalists) or those who, while maintaining both poles of the dilemma, reject attempts to explain their compatibility. (This is a common gambit among contemporary Protestant theologians: when confronted with our question, as the Roman Catholic Joseph Neuner has observed, "they will generally answer that they do not know: it is God's concern, not ours; revelation speaks only about salvation in Jesus Christ."[13])

Two basic types of explanation have been suggested.[14] One of these pictures God's saving work in Jesus Christ as effective for all human beings here and now, within the confines of the present life. The other, in contrast, prefers prospective or eschatological imagery: the eternal destiny of human beings is decided in death or beyond death in the encounter with Jesus who is the life of the world to come. Each of these options can appeal with varying degrees of persuasiveness to early scriptural or patristic motifs, but most later Christians, especially in the West, have refused to adopt either of these two ways of accounting for the salvation of nonbelievers on the grounds that explicit faith in the Triune God and/or membership in the visible church (at least through the "baptism of desire") is necessary now that the truth has been finally revealed in Jesus Christ. Only rarely are those who have never heard the gospel saved, but when this happens, so it was generally explained, it is through a special revelation to those who have not had the opportunity to hear the biblical message. Nevertheless, this theological exclusiveness has not become doctrinally definitive in any of the major Christian traditions and is now, as we have mentioned, widely repudiated. The major doctrinal concern has been to preserve the *Christus solus,* not to deny the possibility of salvation to non-Christians.

The currently most widespread explanation of this possibility is of the first type, and has been developed most fully by two-dimensional experiential-expressivists such as Karl Rahner and Bernard Lonergan. They identify the prereflective, inarticulate experience of the divine, which they hold is at the heart of every religion, with the saving grace of Christ. Those non-Christians who respond to the inward call already share in the same justification, the same salvation, that is at work in Christians even though, unlike Christians, they have no conscious adherence or visible sacramental bond to the historical Jesus Christ who is both the ultimate source and the only fully and finally appropriate objective correlate of their inner experience of salvation. Their faith, one might say, is wholly implicit, yet one may speak of them, Rahner suggests, as "anonymous Christians," for their subjective appropriation of salvation may be as ontologically genuine even in this life as in the case of those who have explicit faith or are manifestly members of the people of God. Thus the *Christus solus* can be reconciled with the salvation of non-Christians.

Neither the classical cognitivists nor those who think of religions in primarily cultural-linguistic terms can adopt this explanation. Cognitivists in the past have often tried to find a general revelation, or a natural theology, or a universal religion of reason sufficient for salvation behind and within all particular religions. They have attempted to reduce the propositional truths that are necessary for salvation to as small a number of "fundamental articles" as possible (e.g., "he that cometh to God must believe that he is, and that he is a rewarder of them that diligently seek him," Heb. 11:6). Then they have argued that acceptance of these truths is equivalent to belief in Christ and can take place apart from historical revelation. These efforts have been widely discredited in the churches, however, because they have often led to deism of the rationalistic Enlightenment variety, and even more because increased modern awareness of historical and cultural relativity has made implausible the notion of propositionally statable truths common to all religions. In our day, those who believe there is a universal religion or revelation behind all religions generally describe it in experiential, not propositional, terms. Thus the only currently available alternative for those of a cultural-linguistic inclination is a prospective theory. It has been proposed that non-Christians can share in the future salvation even though they, unlike those with living Christian faith, have not yet begun to do so. According to this view, saving faith cannot be wholly anonymous, wholly implicit, but must be in some measure explicit: it comes, as Paul puts it, *ex auditu,* from hearing (Rom. 10:17).

The question for us in this section is whether a prospective *fides ex auditu* explanation of the salvation of non-Christians, such as is compatible with (though of course not implied by) a cultural-linguistic outlook, is theologically as tenable as an "anonymous Christian" one. Both options, it seems, can be made consistent with Scripture and tradition and with the contemporary need for interreligious dialogue. The decision between them is likely to depend on the contemporary *Zeitgeist* (i.e., on nontheological factors) and therefore does not affect the issue of the Christian availability of the associated theories of religion.

On the scriptural issue, the prospective *fides ex auditu* option seems to
have the advantage, although it is not a decisive one. In terms of the basic
New Testament eschatological pictures, non-Christians (i.e., Gentiles)
would seem not yet to be confronted by the question of salvation: they are
not heading toward either heaven or hell; they have no future, but are still
trapped in the past, in the darkness of the old aeon. Only through the
message of the coming kingdom, of God's Messiah, does the new age, the
true future of the world, become real for them, and only then does either
final redemption or final damnation become possible. And yet this biblical
preference for eschatological imagery does not exclude (for it does not
envision) the kind of saving implicit faith postulated by the theory of
anonymous Christianity. The decision between these two views depends, it
seems, not on exegesis, but on the systematic historical framework within
which one interprets the biblical data.

The same indecisive conclusion is reached, it seems, if one appeals, not
to the letter of Scripture, but to the fundamental spirit or attitude of the
early Christians toward unbelievers. Christians in the first centuries appear
to have had an extraordinary combination of relaxation and urgency in their
attitude toward those outside the church. On the one hand, they do not
seem to have worried about the ultimate fate of the overwhelming majority
of non-Christians among whom they lived. We hear of no crises of con-
science resulting from the necessity they were often under to conceal the
fact that they were believers even from close friends or kindred. Christians
did not seem to have viewed themselves as watchmen who would be held
guilty of the blood of the pagans they failed to warn—the Old Testament
text refers, after all, to the obligation to admonish, not Gentiles, but those
who are already part of the chosen people (Ezek. 3:18). Yet, on the other
hand, missionary proclamation was urgent and faith and baptism were life
from death: the passage from the old age into the new. From the point of
view of most subsequent theologies, the anomalies and the cognitive dissonance involved in this combination of attitudes would seem to be insupport-
able; and it is therefore at least plausible to suppose that the early Christians
had certain unrecorded convictions that would relieve the tensions about
how God saves unbelievers. One of these convictions, most Protestant and
some Catholic exegetes hold, is perhaps reflected in the reference to Christ
preaching to the souls in prison (I Peter 3:19), and others are suggested in
universalist-sounding biblical texts (e.g., Col. 1:20; Eph. 1:9f.; Phil. 2:10f.;
I Cor. 15:28; I John 2:2; Acts 3:21). By and large, however, it would appear
that these views never became a problem and so remained largely unarticulated. The early Christians both before and after the New Testament
period said too little about these matters to provide a basis for deciding
between our two options or for some other alternative.

It might appear, however, that there are later doctrinal objections to the possibility of a saving encounter with the risen Lord beyond the confines of this present life. One view, first developed by some nineteenth-century Protestant dogmaticians, suggests the possibility of a future state in which unbelievers are given what might be called a "second chance"; but a long tradition (dogmatized on the Catholic side) holds that the ultimate fate of every human being is definitively decided at death. Recently however, Roman Catholic authors, including Karl Rahner,[15] have suggested an interpretation of this view that, somewhat surprisingly, can also be utilized in a prospective *fides ex auditu* approach.

The proposal is that dying itself be pictured as the point at which every human being is ultimately and expressly confronted by the gospel, by the crucified and risen Lord. It is only then that the final decision is made for or against Christ; and this is true, not only of unbelievers but also of believers. All previous decisions, whether for faith or against faith, are preliminary. The final die is cast beyond our space and time, beyond empirical observation, beyond all speculation about "good" or "bad" deaths, when a person loses his or her rootage in this world and passes into the inexpressible transcendence that surpasses all words, images, and thoughts. We must trust and hope, although we cannot know, that in this dreadful yet wondrous end and climax of life no one will be lost. And here, even if not before, the offer of redemption is explicit. Thus it is possible to be hopeful and trusting about the ultimate salvation of non-Christians no less than Christians even if one does not think in terms of a primordial, prereflective experience of Christ's grace.

In reference to interreligious relations, this outlook can be developed in such a way as to oppose the boasting and sense of superiority that destroys the possibility of open and mutually enriching dialogue. One can say that the situation of the Christian is in some respects more, not less, perilous than that of the non-Christian. Judgment begins in the house of the Lord (I Peter 4:17), and many of the first shall be last, and the last first (Matt. 19:30). When one considers these and related passages, one sometimes gets the impression that the Bible balances Cyprian's claim that there is no salvation outside the church *(extra ecclesia nulla salus)* with an at least equally emphatic insistence that the beginning of damnation, of deliberate opposition to God, is possible only within the church, within the people of God: Jesus pronounced his woes (and wept), it will be recalled, over the cities of Israel, not those of the Gentiles. On this view, there is no damnation —just as there is no salvation—outside the church. One must, in other words, learn the language of faith before one can know enough about its message knowingly to reject it and thus be lost.

Perhaps the most important barrier to Christian boasting within this perspective, however, is that when the *fides ex auditu* is emphasized, then explicit faith is understood, not as expressing or articulating the existential depths, but rather as producing and forming them. For Christians, even mature Christians, this process has just begun. They have only begun to confess Jesus as Lord, to speak the Christian language, the language of the coming kingdom. Their thoughts, volitions, and affections are just beginning to be conformed to the One who is the express image of the Father (Heb. 1:3). The Holy Spirit which is in them is the pledge of, not the participation in, future glory. They have not yet learned to love God above all things and their neighbors as themselves, for this is what comes at the end of the road in eschatological fulfillment. What distinguishes their love from that of the non-Christian is, not its present subjective quality, but rather the fact that it is beginning to be shaped by the message of Jesus' cross and resurrection. Only at the end of the road, only in the eschatological fulfillment, will they have truly learned to love God above all things and their neighbors as themselves.

In this perspective, experiential-expressivist descriptions of implicit faith are far too glorious even for the *fides ex auditu* and must rather be applied to ultimate completion when faith passes into the beatific vision. Only then, in the murky and untamed depths of their beings, will Christians (as Rahner puts it) experience and accept the abysmal mystery on which they are grounded, "not as consuming judgment, but as fulfilling nearness,"[16] or (as Lonergan says) be "unrestrictedly in love."[17] In short, every aspect of the new life exists in the modality of hope. This is why (as Luther put it) "we do not yet have our goodness *in re,* but *in fide et spe.*"[18] This also is why pride in being a Christian is excluded. Believers have by grace just begun to learn of the one in whom alone is salvation, but in moral and religious quality they are like other human beings, worse than some and better than others.

In answer to objections that this makes salvation merely fictive or imaginary, not ontologically real, it can be said, to use a simile, that those who have turned around may be standing shoulder to shoulder with their neighbors and yet be living in light rather than darkness, dawn rather than night, the beginning of the new age, not the end of the old. Speaking in more complex terms, the metaphor of a child learning a language is useful. The content of what is said by toddlers is very much the same whether they speak a primitive or a modern tongue. In both cases they express the same elementary needs and reactions in basically the same world of objects to be enjoyed or avoided and of persons to be trusted or feared. But one language may in the long run open up all the riches of human history and of a vastly promising though ominous future, while the other, the better a child learns it, imprisons him more tightly in his little tribe or village. At two years of age, the member of a preliterate culture might still be a potential Confucius, Newton, or Beethoven; at twenty, never.

In terms of this analogy, all human beings are toddlers, whether Peter, or Paul, or the veriest infant in Christ. The decisive question regarding them is whether the language they have begun to learn *ex auditu* is that of Jesus Christ, that of true humanity, or something else. Is, for example, the love about which they feebly stutter, and which they are just beginning to understand and hope for, defined by Jesus' life, death, and resurrection, or in some other way?

In any case it is ridiculous for Christians to boast. They are like infants mouthing scraps out of Shakespeare or the *Principia Mathematica,* parrot-like, by rote. Only occasionally do they have inklings of the meanings of the words they utter. Thus, there is even less reason for boasting in this perspective than if salvation can be by implicit without explicit faith.

This inference, so it can be argued, is reinforced when one thinks of the temptation to religious pretentiousness or imperialism implicit in the notion that non-Christians are anonymously Christian. There is something arrogant about supposing that Christians know what nonbelievers experience and believe in the depths of their beings better than they know themselves, and that therefore the task of dialogue or evangelism is to increase their self-awareness. The communication of the gospel is not a form of psychotherapy, but rather the offer and the act of sharing one's own beloved language—the language that speaks of Jesus Christ—with all those who are interested, in the full awareness that God does not call all to be part of the witnessing people.

This view of the salvation of non-Christians seems wholly compatible with what was said in the previous section about the need for dialogue and cooperation with other religions. To hold that a particular language is the only one that has the words and concepts that can authentically speak of the ground of being, the goal of history, and true humanity (for Christians believe they cannot genuinely speak of these apart from telling and retelling the biblical story) is not at all the same as denying that other religions have resources for speaking truths and referring to realities, even highly important truths and realities, of which Christianity as yet knows nothing and by which it could be greatly enriched. Whatever the faults of Hellenization, for example, it must be seen as a process in which Christians learned much of inestimable value from ancient paganisms and from the cultures and philosophies that were their offspring. This process of learning needs to be continued in reference to contemporary non-Christian religions and cultures. Conversely, one of the ways in which Christians can serve their neighbors may be through helping adherents of other religions to purify and enrich their heritages, to make them better speakers of the languages they have. It can be argued that this is a sounder basis for dialogue than when one seeks to find the grace of Christ at work in non-Christian religions. The danger in doing the latter need not be that of denying the *solus Christus,* but rather of failing to do justice to non-Christian truths and values.

We come now to what is perhaps the major difficulty with the alternative we are examining. Its prospective reference seems mythological or unreal to those who think science or philosophy makes it impossible to affirm a temporally and objectively future eschaton.

The difficulty with this as an argument, however, is that the notions of an anonymously Christian preconceptual and prelinguistic experience of salvation seems equally unreal and mythological to those who think in cultural-linguistic terms. Their picture of a religion, as we have said before in somewhat different terms, is that of a system of discursive and nondiscursive symbols linking motivation and action and providing an ultimate legitimation for basic patterns of thought, feeling, and behavior uniquely characteristic of a given community or society and its members.[19] For them, religions are not expressions of the transcendental heights and depths of human experience, but are rather patterns of ritual, myth, belief, and conduct which constitute, rather than being constituted by, that which modern people often think of as most profound in human beings, viz., their existential self-understanding. This model of the human being, to repeat, is the inverse of the experiential-expressive one. The humanly real, one might say, is not constructed from below upward or from the inner to the outer, but from the outer to the inner, and from above downward. The acquisition of a language—necessarily from the outside—is a "jump which was the coming into being of man."[20] All the heights and depths of human knowledge, faith, and love are the effects and not the causes of the skill (whose acquisition is largely beyond conscious control) with which men and women learn to use their cultural and linguistic resources. The Christian theological application of this view is that just as an individual becomes human by learning a language, so he or she begins to become a new creature through hearing and interiorizing the language that speaks of Christ. Admittedly the patterns impressed by a religion may become latent in a community or individual in the form of generalized attitudes and sentiments that are no longer supported by the original rituals and beliefs. Thus a post-Christian society can still be in one sense Christian, but this latent Christianity could have no other origins than in the explicit form of the religion.[21] The notion of an anonymous Christianity present in the depths of other religions is from this perspective nonsense, and a theory of the salvation of non-Christians built upon it seems thoroughly unreal.

There is no specifically theological way of deciding between these competing charges of unreality. They are in part dependent on different philosophical orientations. One of these is the Continental tradition of idealism, romanticism, and phenomenological existentialism, while the other is the more empiricist Anglo-American outlook (which also, it can be argued, has affinities to premodern Aristotelian and Thomistic thought rather than to the more mystical Platonic and Augustinian currents). Even more fundamental are psychosocial influences. The sense of what is real or unreal is in large part socially constructed, and what seems credible or incredible to contemporary theologians is likely to be more the product of their milieu and intellectual conditioning than of their science, philosophy, or theological argumentation. All that can be said in conclusion, therefore, is that mythological elements (in the technical, nonpejorative sense of "myth") are indispensable in any religion, and that the salvation of non-Christians in the eschatological future makes at least as much theological sense as the myth of a primordial, prelinguistic experience of the *gratia Christi.* If so, there is no reason for choosing between theories of religion on the basis of this particular theological issue. The possibility of the salvation of non-Christians—while maintaining the *solus Christus*—can be affirmed with equal plausibility (or implausibility) from either an anonymous Christian or an eschatologically futuristic perspective.[22]

IV
EXCURSUS ON RELIGION AND TRUTH

Other issues remain, however, and of these the major one for this chapter is that of the relation of religion and truth claims. If we are to do justice to the actual speech and practice of religious people, we must go farther than in our earlier discussion of unsurpassability. We must not simply allow for the possibility that a religion may be categorially as well as symbolically or expressively true; we must also allow for its possible propositional truth. Christians, for example, generally act as if an affirmation such as "Jesus Christ is Lord" is more than a categorial truth: Not only do the stories about Jesus define a singular concept of Lordship (including as it does a unique notion of "nonmasochistic" suffering and obedient servanthood); but this concept of Lordship—so a theology of the cross maintains—is alone adequate to what is indeed most lordly in reality. Nor do Christians stop with symbolic truth, viz., the claim that these stories can efficaciously express and communicate the genuine lordliness that Tillich calls "the power of the New Being"; but they go on and assert that it is propositionally true that Christ is Lord: i.e., the particular individual of which the stories are told is, was, and will be definitively and unsurpassably the Lord. The great strength of a cognitive-propositional theory of religion is that, unlike a purely experiential-expressive one, it admits the possibility of such truth claims, and a crucial theological challenge to a cultural-linguistic approach is whether it also can do so. The discussion of this challenge will inevitably be somewhat technical.

We need, first, to distinguish between what I shall call the "intrasystematic" and the "ontological" truth of statements. The first is the truth of coherence; the second, that truth of correspondence to reality which, according to epistemological realists, is attributable to first-order propositions. Utterances are intrasystematically true when they cohere with the total relevant context, which, in the case of a religion when viewed in cultural-linguistic terms, is not only other utterances but also the correlative forms of life. Thus for a Christian, "God is Three and One," or "Christ is Lord" are true only as parts of a total pattern of speaking, thinking, feeling, and acting. They are false when their use in any given instance is inconsistent with what the pattern as a whole affirms of God's being and will. The crusader's battle cry *"Christus est Dominus,"* for example, is false when used to authorize cleaving the skull of the infidel (even though the same words in other contexts may be a true utterance). When thus employed, it contradicts the Christian understanding of Lordship as embodying, for example, suffering servanthood.

All this is simply to say that coherence is necessary for truth in nonreligious as well as religious domains. For example, a demonstration in Euclidean geometry which implies that parallel lines eventually meet must be false for formally the same reason that the crusader's cry must be false: the statements in both cases are intrasystematically inconsistent. The difference is that in the Christian case the system is constituted, not in purely intellectual terms by axioms, definitions, and corollaries, but by a set of stories used in specifiable ways to interpret and live in the world. The mistake of a primarily cognitive-propositional theory of religion, from a cultural-linguistic perspective, is to overlook this difference. It is unable to do justice to the fact that a religious system is more like a natural language than a formally organized set of explicit statements, and that the right use of this language, unlike a mathematical one, cannot be detached from a particular way of behaving. And yet, once these differences are taken into account, it is important to remember that a religion, like a mathematical system, seeks to be a coherent whole within which, therefore, the intrasystematic truth or falsity of particular utterances is of fundamental significance.

For epistemological realists, intrasystematic truth or falsity is fundamental in the sense that it is a necessary though not sufficient condition for the second kind of truth: that of ontological correspondence. A statement, in other words, cannot be ontologically true unless it is intrasystematically true, but intrasystematic truth is quite possible without ontological truth. An intrasystematically true statement is ontologically false—or, more accurately, meaningless—if it is part of a system that lacks the concepts or categories to refer to the relevant realities, but it is ontologically true if it is part of a system that is itself categorially true (adequate). The geometric analogy holds at this point also. If space is in fact Euclidean rather than Reimannian or Lobachevskian, then statements that depend on the parallel-lines axiom are ontologically true (which, under the influence of relativity theory, we now generally believe they are not). Similarly, if the form of life and understanding of the world shaped by an authentic use of the Christian stories does in fact correspond to God's being and will, then the proper use of *Christus est Dominus* is not only intrasystematically but also ontologically true. Utterances within any not totally incoherent religion can on this account be intrasystematically true, but this in no sense assures their ontological truth or meaningfulness. Similarly, to cite yet another parallel, the statement "Denmark is the land where Hamlet lived" is intrasystematically true within the context of Shakespeare's play, but this implies nothing regarding ontological truth or falsity unless the play is taken as history. To repeat, intrasystematic truth is a necessary but not sufficient condition for ontological truth.

The ontological truth of religious utterances, like their intrasystematic truth, is different as well as similar to what holds in other realms of discourse. Their correspondence to reality in the view we are expounding is not an attribute that they have when considered in and of themselves, but is only a function of their role in constituting a form of life, a way of being in the world, which itself corresponds to the Most Important, the Ultimately Real. Medieval scholastics spoke of truth as an adequation of the mind to the thing *(adaequatio mentis ad rem),* but in the religious domain, this mental isomorphism of the knowing and the known can be pictured as part and parcel of a wider conformity of the self to God. The same point can be made by means of J. L. Austin's notion of a "performatory" use of language:[23] a religious utterance, one might say, acquires the propositional truth of ontological correspondence only insofar as it is a performance, an act or deed, which helps create that correspondence.

This admittedly does not happen in nonreligious performative speech, where, at least normally, utterances cannot simultaneously function both performatively and propositionally. To say, for example, that marriage vows are performative, i.e., create the reality of marriage, is to deny that they are propositional, i.e., correspond to a prior reality of marriage. Yet, if the banality may be permitted, in a marriage genuinely made in heaven, the earthly promises would produce a "propositional" correspondence of one reality to another. If this example has any merit, it suggests one way in which a statement can be conceived of as having the propositional force of an ontological truth claim about objective reality even though it does not fit the classical model of a proposition as an *adaequatio mentis ad rem.*

This is not the place to pursue in detail the logical issues raised by truth claims in religion, but it is crucial for our argument to ask whether the picture we have sketched does justice to what religious people themselves maintain. Paul, for example, tells us that no one can say "Jesus is Lord" except by the Holy Spirit (I Cor. 12:3); and Luther frequently insists in a similar vein that I cannot genuinely affirm that Christ is "the Lord" unless I thereby make him "my Lord."[24] These statements are difficult to accommodate if one holds with cognitivists that the meaning, truth, and falsity of propositions are independent of the subjective dispositions of those who utter them; but the alternative experiential-expressive interpretation which reduces the religious significance of such statements as "Jesus is Lord" to their role of symbolizing inner experiences or existential orientations seems at least equally unacceptable. Paul and Luther, at any rate, quite clearly believed that Christ's Lordship is objectively real no matter what the faith or unfaith of those who hear or say the words. What they were concerned to assert is that the only way to assert this truth is to do something about it, i.e., to commit oneself to a way of life; and this concern, it would seem, is wholly congruent with the suggestion that it is only through the performatory use of religious utterances that they acquire propositional force.

Yet this performatory conformity of the self to God can also be pictured in epistemologically realistic fashion as involving a correspondence of the mind to divine reality. This is true, at any rate, when one conceives of this correspondence in as limited a fashion as does, for example, Thomas Aquinas. There seems to be no reason, in other words, why cultural-linguistic theories of religion need exclude, even though they do not imply, the modest cognitivism or propositionalism represented by at least some classical theists, of whom Aquinas is a good example.

Aquinas holds that although in statements about God the human mode of signifying *(modus significandi)* does not correspond to anything in the divine being, the signified *(significatum)* does.[25] Thus, for example, when we say that God is good, we do not affirm that any of our concepts of goodness *(modi significandi)* apply to him, but rather that there is a concept of goodness unavailable to us, viz., God's understanding of his own goodness, which does apply. What we assert, in other words, is that " 'God is good' is meaningful and true," but without knowing the meaning of 'God is good.'[26] Somewhat similarly, nonphysicists who do not know enough mathematics to understand the theory of relativity may rightly assert the truth of "Space-time is a four-dimensional continuum," without knowing the sense in which this statement is true or even meaningful. Both they and theologians may use analogies to exclude erroneous interpretations, but they are only able to specify how these predications cannot correspond, not how they do correspond to reality (or, as a modern might say, how they are falsifiable), and therefore are unable to affirm them together with their *modi significandi*). Yet, despite this informational vacuity, the *significata* can be affirmed: it is possible to claim that the intellectual judgments "God is good" or "Space-time is a four-dimensional continuum" refer or correspond to objective realities even when one cannot specify the *modi significandi* by offering, e.g., a falsifiable description of God's goodness or of a four-dimensional space-time continuum.

What, however, is the function of truth claims about God if their cognitive content is as minimal as has just been suggested? If we do not know how God is good (viz., the *modus significandi*), then we cannot derive any nontautologous consequences from the affirmation that he is good. Here, so it can be suggested, classical theists can usefully appeal for their purposes to the performative function of religious utterances which was earlier mentioned. They might say that, despite its informational vacuity, the claim that God truly is good in himself is of utmost importance because it authorizes responding as if he were good in the ways indicated by the stories of creation, providence, and redemption which shape believers' thoughts and actions; or, to put the same point in another way, seriously to commit oneself to thinking and acting as if God were good in relation to us *(quoad nos)* in the ways indicated by the stories involves asserting that he really is good in himself *(in se)* even though, as the canonical texts testify, the meaning of this latter claim is utterly beyond human comprehension.

Similarly, to cite a logically more complex case, the *significatum* of the claim that Jesus truly and objectively was raised from the dead provides the warrant for behaving in the ways recommended by the resurrection stories even when one grants the impossibility of specifying the mode in which those stories signify.[27] Admittedly, this second example, though not the first, goes beyond anything Aquinas says, but there seems to be no reason for not applying the distinction between the *modus significandi* and the *significatum* and the notion of analogical knowledge to resurrection (and creation, consummation, etc.) as well as to the being of God *in se*. In any event, when propositionalism becomes as modest as in this "agnostic"[28] reading of Thomas Aquinas, it is no longer incompatible with the kind of "performative-propositional" theological theory of religious truth that fits a cultural-linguistic approach.

In order to round out this sketch, it is desirable to enlarge briefly on the commonplace that sentences are not to be identified with propositions: different sentences can make one and the same affirmation about reality, and, more important for our immediate purposes, the same sentence may be used either propositionally or nonpropositionally. The sentence "This car is red," as it occurs on this page, for example, cannot be a proposition, for it specifies no particular auto and no particular time before or after which the vehicle might be of a different color: it can be neither true nor false. The same point holds *mutatis mutandis* for religious sentences: they acquire enough referential specificity to have first-order or ontological truth or falsity only in determinate settings, and this rarely if ever happens on the pages of theological treatises or in the course of doctrinal discussions. The theological and doctrinal uses of, e.g., "Christ is Lord" are important (as we shall have occasion to observe at greater length in the next two chapters), but they are not propositional. For Christian theological purposes, that sentence becomes a first-order proposition capable (so nonidealists would say) of making ontological truth claims only as it is used in the activities of adoration, proclamation, obedience, promise-hearing, and promise-keeping which shape individuals and communities into conformity to the mind of Christ.

If this is so, there is a sense in which those unskilled in the language of faith not only fail to affirm but also cannot deny that "Jesus is Lord." The reasons for this are formally similar to those which make it impossible to deny the statement "This car is red" unless one knows the circumstances —for example, the parking lot, ostensively indicated vehicle, and particular time—in which the sentence was uttered. One must be, so to speak, inside the relevant context; and in the case of a religion, this means that one must have some skill in *how* to use its language and practice its way of life before the propositional meaning of its affirmations becomes determinate enough to be rejected.

This discussion of propositions, it is scarcely necessary to point out, supports the theological proposal in the previous section regarding the salvation of adherents of other religions: nonbelievers are not yet confronted by the question of salvation because it is only by acquiring some familiarity with the determinate settings in which religious utterances acquire propositional force that one can grasp their meaning well enough genuinely to reject (or accept) them. Similarly, this account may help explain why apostasy is generally regarded as more serious than refusal of faith. The nonbeliever, however well-informed about the symbolic vocabulary and conceptual syntax of a religion, can be presumed, in the absence of actual practice, not to understand its propositional claims, but it is harder to make a similar presumption in favor of the apostate.

In conclusion, a religion can be interpreted as possibly containing ontologically true affirmations, not only in cognitivist theories but also in cultural-linguistic ones. There is nothing in the cultural-linguistic approach that requires the rejection (or the acceptance) of the epistemological realism and correspondence theory of truth, which, according to most of the theological tradition, is implicit in the conviction of believers that when they rightly use a sentence such as "Christ is Lord" they are uttering a true first-order proposition.

Nevertheless, the conditions under which propositions can be uttered are very different in cognitivist and cultural-linguistic approaches: they are located on quite different linguistic strata. For the cognitivist, it is chiefly technical theology and doctrine which are propositional, while on the alternate model, propositional truth and falsity characterize ordinary religious language when it is used to mold lives through prayer, praise, preaching, and exhortation. It is only on this level that human beings linguistically exhibit their truth or falsity, their correspondence or lack of correspondence to the Ultimate Mystery. Technical theology and official doctrine, in contrast, are second-order discourse about the first-intentional uses of religious language. Here, in contrast to the common supposition, one rarely if ever succeeds in making affirmations with ontological import, but rather engages in explaining, defending, analyzing, and regulating the liturgical, kerygmatic, and ethical modes of speech and action within which such affirmations from time to time occur. Just as grammar by itself affirms nothing either true or false regarding the world in which language is used, but only about language, so theology and doctrine, to the extent that they are second-order activities, assert nothing either true or false about God and his relation to creatures, but only speak about such assertions. These assertions, in turn, cannot be made except when speaking religiously, i.e., when seeking to align oneself and others performatively with what one takes to be most important in the universe by worshiping, promising, obeying, exhorting, preaching.

This brings us to our next major problem area, that of church doctrines. We have argued in this chapter that a cultural-linguistic approach is compatible with strong and not only weak positions on unsurpassability, interreligious dialogue, the salvation of non-Christians, and the propositional truth of religious affirmations, but yet a problem remains: the role that most Christian traditions have historically assigned to church doctrines seems imperiled. If these are not first-order propositions, what are they? Can they be construed nonpropositionally (as a cultural-linguistic outlook suggests they ought to be), while at the same time allowing for their possible permanence and normativeness, and for the possible infallibility of the teaching function of the church? These and comparable questions are not urgent in most religions, but they are of great intra-Christian importance. The ecumenical availability of a cultural-linguistic approach depends in large part on whether these questions can be successfully answered, and it is to them that we turn in the next two chapters.

NOTES

1. For an interpretation of the statements of Vatican II on these matters, see George Lindbeck, *The Future of Roman Catholic Theology* (Fortress Press, 1970), esp. pp. 27–38.

2. Bernard Lonergan, *Insight* (Harper & Row, 1978), p. 399.

3. Not only those in the tradition of Pascal, but also Thomas Aquinas can be cited in favor of this point: "Unbelievers do not 'believe that there is a God' in the sense in which this can be regarded as an act of faith. They do not believe that God exists under the conditions which faith defines. Hence they do not really believe that there is a God" (*ST* II-II.2.2, ad 3). For an interpretation of Aquinas which stresses this "Pascalian" moment in his thought, see Victor Preller, *Divine Science and the Science of God* (Princeton University Press, 1967).

4. See Per Eric Persson, *Sacra Doctrina: Reason and Revelation in Aquinas,* tr. by J. A. R. Mackenzie (Oxford: Basil Blackwell, 1970), for an account of the *revelabilia.*

5. To be sure, patristic and medieval authors recommended "despoiling the Egyptians," but they thought of this as a borrowing from the philosophy rather than from the religion of the pagans.

6. Maurice Wiles, "Looking Into the Sun," in his *Working Papers in Doctrine* (London: SCM Press, 1976), pp. 148–163, esp. 156–157.

7. Bernard Lonergan, *Method in Theology* (Herder & Herder, 1972), p. 304.

8. John Bowker speaks of religions as "route-finding activities" in *The Sense of God* (Oxford: Clarendon Press, 1973), pp. 82ff., 86ff.

9. Rudolf Otto, *Mysticism East and West* (Macmillan Co., 1932), remains an excellent account of the similarities (and, though not to the same extent, of the differences) between Eckhart and Shankara.

10. I am here using "authenticity" without the technical meaning of "self-transcendence" that it has in much modern thought. Cf. Lonergan, *Method in Theology,* p. 104.

11. "Let Christians, while witnessing to their own faith and way of life, acknowledge, preserve and encourage the spiritual and moral truths found among non-Christians." (*Nostra Aetate* [Declaration on the Relation of the Church to Non-Christian Religions] 2, *The Documents of Vatican II,* ed. by Austin P. Flannery [Pillar Books, 1975], p. 739.) It should be emphasized that the nature of the possible assistance will vary because of the differences in the relations between the various religions. It is widely argued, for example, that the logic of the biblical narratives leads to the conclusion (usually denied in Christian history) that Israel and Gentile Christianity are parts of the one people of God and will retain their respective identities (though, it may be hoped, not their past or present relations) until the end (Romans 9–11). The task of the Gentile church is "to stir Israel to emulation" (Rom. 11:11), and it can be inferred that the Jews may at times have a similar role vis-à-vis Gentile Christians (Rom. 11:19–24). While analogues of this relation could also obtain with other non-Christian religions, they would, within most theological frameworks, be rather distant ones. For a survey of the politically most salient

Christian theological views of Jewish-Christian relations, see George Lindbeck, "Christians Between Arabs and Jews," *Worldview* 22/9 (Sept. 1979), pp. 25–39.

12. For a development of this idea of the "providential diversity of religions," see Joseph DiNoia, "The Universality of Salvation and the Diversity of Religious Aims," *Worldmission* 32 (Winter 1981–82), pp. 4–15.

13. Joseph Neuner, *Christian Revelation and World Religions* (London: Burns & Oats, 1967), p. 10.

14. For literature relevant to pp. 56–59, see George Lindbeck, *"Fides ex Auditu* and the Salvation of Non-Christians: Contemporary Catholic and Protestant Positions," *The Gospel and the Ambiguity of the Church*, ed. by V. Vajta (Fortress Press, 1974), pp. 91–123.

15. Karl Rahner, *On the Theology of Death,* tr. by Charles H. Henkey (Herder & Herder, 1961). The argument is that in his death—in his "descent into hell," Christ became "the heart of the world, the innermost center of creation" (pp. 71–74). The very act of dying is an encounter with God which makes a person's decision for or against God, foreshadowed during the time of his or her bodily life, final and unalterable (p. 35).

16. Karl Rahner, *Theological Investigations,* Vol. 5 (Helicon Press, 1966), p. 7.

17. Lonergan, *Method in Theology,* p. 122 and passim.

18. Martin Luther, *WA* 4.147.23ff. (scholion to Ps. 101:3); cf. *Lectures on Romans,* tr. and ed. by Wilhelm Pauck (Westminster Press, 1961), p. 127 (*WA* 56.272.16f.).

19. Clifford Geertz, *The Interpretation of Cultures* (Basic Books, 1973), p. 90.

20. Wilfrid Sellars, *Science, Perception, and Reality* (London: Routledge & Kegan Paul, 1963), p. 6.

21. Paul Tillich, *Systematic Theology,* Vol. 3 (University of Chicago Press, 1963), p. 246, has a rather different view of "latency." For him it can be a preparation for, as well as a consequence of, manifest religion.

22. The work of Teilhard de Chardin illustrates that modern scientific cosmologies (except for the oscillating universe variety) differ from all previous ones in Christian history (from Ptolemy and Aristotle to Einstein) in being congenial to a futuristic eschatology; but, as is indicated in the last chapter of this book, theologians should be more wary than was Teilhard in basing theological conclusions on presumed scientific evidence. Attempts to show that a science or philosophy can be given an interpretation consistent with a religion (for example, Aquinas' interpretation of Aristotle) may at times be laudable, but that is different from making science or philosophy foundational.

23. John L. Austin, "Performative Utterances," in his *Philosophical Papers,* 2d ed. (Oxford: Clarendon Press, 1970), pp. 232–252. Cf. his *How to Do Things with Words* (Oxford: Clarendon Press, 1962).

24. For this particular use of the *pro me,* see Ian Siggins, *Martin Luther's Doctrine of Christ* (Yale University Press, 1970), pp. 181f.

25. Aquinas, *ST* I.13.3; *CG* I.30.

26. For interpretations of Aquinas similar to this, see David Burrell, *Aquinas: God and Action* (University of Notre Dame Press, 1979), pp. 8–10 and passim; also his

Analogy and Philosophical Language (Yale University Press, 1973), pp. 136–139. Cf. also Victor Preller, n. 3, above. In the background of Preller's interpretation is the work of Wilfrid Sellars (n. 20, above).

27. For additional comments on this way of looking at the resurrection, see George Lindbeck (together with G. Baum and R. McBrien) in John Kirvan (ed.), *The Infallibility Debate* (Paulist Press, 1971), pp. 132–133.

28. Staunch traditional Thomists have been among those who speak of Thomas' "agnosticism." See, e.g., Antonin Sertillanges, *S. Thomas d'Aquin* (Paris: Alcan, 1925).

CHAPTER 4

THEORIES OF DOCTRINE

The theory of church doctrine provides the critical test for the theological and ecumenical usefulness of cultural-linguistic approaches to religion. What kind of meaning can such approaches give to the notion that doctrines are not only normative but permanent? Most Christian traditions have held that their doctrines have this character, and Roman Catholicism in addition maintains that its teaching office when making *de fide* pronouncements is infallible. If the regulative or rule theory appropriate to cultural and linguistic models excludes these claims of normativeness, permanence, and infallibility, it is theologically useless for many theologians and ecumenically useless for all.

This chapter concludes, as could be expected, that a rule theory not only is doctrinally possible but has advantages over other positions. Admittedly the proof is far from rigorous. As is generally true in debates between fundamentally different outlooks, there is no neutral point of view from which to adjudicate differences. The outlooks themselves shape the criteria and skew the evidence in their own favor. Yet I hope at least to show that a rule theory is a serious option for theologians in the historic Christian mainstream, not only for nontheological students of religion.

The first task will be to identify the problems that theories of doctrine must consider. We shall turn, second, to the exposition of rule theory with special reference to the problem of religious and doctrinal constancy and change, and, third, to different types of of doctrine. The next chapter applies the rule theory to selected examples of controverted doctrine and discusses the major divergences of a rule theory from alternative interpretations.

I
DOCTRINES AND THEIR PROBLEMS

A brief and, if possible, noncontroversial description of doctrines will suffice to pose the problems with which theories must deal.[1] Church doctrines are communally authoritative teachings regarding beliefs and practices that are considered essential to the identity or welfare of the group in question. They may be formally stated or informally operative, but in any case they indicate what constitutes faithful adherence to a community. To disagree with Methodist, Quaker, or Roman Catholic doctrine indicates that one is not a "good" Methodist, Quaker, or Roman Catholic. Someone who opposes pacifism, for example, will not be regarded as fully what a member of the Society of Friends should be. If this conclusion is not drawn, it is evident that the belief has ceased to be communally formative, and it is therefore no longer an operational doctrine even though it may continue to be a formal or official one. In any case, operative doctrines, even if not official ones, are necessary to communal identity. A religious body cannot exist as a recognizably distinctive collectivity unless it has some beliefs and/or practices by which it can be identified.

In order to be clear on the implications of this description, some points need to be elaborated. First, in reference to the inescapability of doctrine, it would seem that the "creedless Christianity" professed by a number of groups (including, for example, many Quakers and the Disciples of Christ) is not genuinely creedless. When creedlessness is insisted on as a mark of group identity, it becomes by definition operationally creedal. Indeed, usually it becomes at least semiofficial, as in the slogan used by some Protestants, "No creed but the Bible." What this aphorism is directed against is not doctrines in general, but postbiblical doctrines—or, more precisely, the official status of these doctrines. (Most biblicistic Protestants, for example, adhere in practice to postbiblical Trinitarianism: they do not deny what the Nicene Creed teaches, but they ignore the creed itself and act as if its teachings were self-evidently scriptural.)

A second point that needs elaboration is the distinction between operational and official doctrines. We have just noted that Nicene Trinitarianism may cease to be official while remaining operational, as in some biblicistic Protestantism, but the converse may also occur: it may cease to be operational while remaining official, as in much liberal Protestantism. In addition, many doctrines remain operational without ever becoming official. This can happen either because they seem so explicitly self-evident that no church has ever felt the need to dogmatize them ("God is love" might serve as a Christian example) or because, although implicit in the larger religious scheme, they remain unrecognized (as was true for long centuries of the Christian opposition to slavery, which has only in relatively recent times been widely acknowledged as communally obligatory, as having doctrinal status).

A third point is that controversy is the normal means whereby implicit doctrines become explicit, and operational ones official. For the most part, only when disputes arise about what it is permissible to teach or practice does a community make up its collective mind and formally make a doctrinal decision. The Marian dogmas of 1854 and 1950 are almost unique in being apparent exceptions to this generalization (for only their definibility, not their truth, was openly contested by Roman Catholics at the time of their promulgation), but one major inciting factor even here, so it can be argued, was the desire to emphasize Roman distinctiveness against what was seen at the time as an especially threatening world. In any case, insofar as official doctrines are the products of conflict, there are two important consequences: first, they must be understood in terms of what they oppose (it is usually much easier to specify what they deny than what they affirm); and, second, the official doctrines of a community may poorly reflect its most important and abiding orientations or beliefs, either because some of the latter may never have been seriously challenged (and therefore never officially defined) or because points that are under most circumstances trivial may on occasion become matters of life and death.

This last point, it is worth noting, has long been recognized. Luther, for example, once said: "If I profess with the loudest voice and clearest exposition every portion of the truth of God except precisely that little point which the world and the devil are at that moment attacking, I am not confessing Christ, however boldly I may be professing Christ. Where the battle rages, there the loyalty of the soldier is proved. To be steady on all battle fronts besides is mere flight and disgrace if he flinches at that point."[2]

Cardinal Newman expressed the same insight rather more diffusely and abstractly, but also using militaristic metaphors: "Nothing is so frivolous and so unphilosophical as the ridicule bestowed on the contest for retaining or surrendering a rite or an observance, such as the use of the Cross in Baptism or the posture of kneeling at the Lord's Table. As well might satire be directed against the manoeuvre of two generals concerning some small portion of ground. The Rubicon was a narrow stream. A slight advantage gained is often at once an omen and a measure of ultimate victory. Political parties, to look at the matter on the lowest ground, are held together by what are the veriest of trifles. An accidental badge, or an inconsistency, may embody the principle and be the seat of life of a party. A system must be looked at as a whole; and may as little admit of mending or altering as an individual. We cannot change one joint of our body for a better; nor can we with impunity open one vein. These analogies must not of course be pressed too far; but they apply far more to morals and politics than theorists of this day are willing to believe. It is remarkable how hidden, as well as insignificant, are these depositories and treasure houses of our most important habits."[3]

The history of doctrine, and not only of politics and morals, is replete with illustrations of Newman's thesis. Gibbon scoffed at the iota that separated the Nicene *homoousios* from the semi-Arian *homoiousios*.[4] He saw only its insignificance, and not that its absence signaled (for the orthodox) one of the "depositories and treasure houses of our most important habits" of faith. Struggles over vestments and images in the sixteenth century functioned similarly; and in our own day, the question of whether to use exclusively masculine pronouns in referring to God has, rightly or wrongly, become profoundly important. These in themselves may be trivial matters, and yet decisions about them can be of crucial significance because of the "important habits," the often implicit operational doctrines, of which they are the depositories.

This brings us to a fourth point, viz., the distinction between theology and doctrine. That they are different is evident: there can be great variety in the theological explanation, communication, and defense of the faith within a framework of communal doctrinal agreement. Those who agree on explicitly formulated doctrines may disagree sharply on how to interpret, justify, or defend them. Conversely, a large measure of consensus on theology can cross confessional divides. Theology and doctrine, to be sure, are normally correlated; and yet it is possible for Catholics and Protestants, for example, to share an Erasmian (or, at almost the opposite extreme, a Barthian) theological outlook while yet remaining doctrinally divided on sacraments and church order.[5] Most of the books entitled "church doctrine" or "church dogmatics," it should be noted, are in fact wide-ranging theological treatises rather than being concerned simply with the doctrines of the churches in the narrow sense in which we are using the term. They generally deal with everything that it is desirable to teach rather than only with that which functions as communally essential; and the explanations, justifications, and defenses of doctrine that they present are optional theological theories rather than communally normative. This distinction between theology and church doctrine is more often adverted to by Roman Catholics than by Protestants,[6] but it is not in itself controversial. Like the three previous points—the impossibility of a creedless religious community, the distinction between operational and official doctrines, and the role of controversy in the articulation of doctrine—it is part of a generally acceptable description of what doctrines are rather than of a distinctive theory about them.

Before turning to theoretical questions about the nature of doctrine, we must say a word about the difficulty in our day of taking doctrines seriously enough to try to understand them.

The modern mood is antipathetic to the very notion of communal norms.[7] This antipathy can be construed, as it is by sociologists of knowledge, as the product of such factors as religious and ideological pluralism and social mobility. When human beings are insistently exposed to conflicting and changing views, they tend to lose their confidence in any of them. Doctrines no longer represent objective realities and are instead experienced as expressions of personal preference: some people have an affinity for Buddhism and others for Christianity, some for Catholicism and others for Protestantism; but as long as each person is honest and sincere, it makes no real difference which faith they embrace. Inevitably in this kind of atmosphere, communal loyalties weaken and are replaced by an emphasis on individual freedom, autonomy, and authenticity. The suggestion that communities have the right to insist on standards of belief and practice as conditions of membership is experienced as an intolerable infringement of the liberty of the self. This reaction is intensified by the growing contradiction between traditional standards and the prevailing values of the wider society as communicated by education, the mass media, and personal contacts. The very words "doctrine" and "dogma" have the smell of the ghetto about them, and to take them seriously is, it seems, to cut oneself off from the larger world. One way to escape from this dilemma is to argue that the (from the modern perspective) absurd doctrines of the past never were important in themselves, but were only expressive symbolizations of deeper experiences and orientations that ought now to be articulated in other and more contemporary ways.[8] Thus an experiential-expressive approach to religion can be easily, though not necessarily, used to legitimate the religious privatism and subjectivism that is fostered by the social pressures of the day. The tendency, when this happens, is to consign all historic doctrines indiscriminately to the junk pile of outgrown superstitions. God himself becomes a discardable item, as for some "death of God" theologians of the 1960s, even among those who continue to think of themselves as Christians. This particular extreme has lost popularity, but the accommodation to culture that it manifested remains powerful in current religious thought; although now, in part under the influence of new gospels from the East, the accommodationism tends to be more proreligious and less secular than a decade or two ago.

The urge to accommodate can be countered in part by the recognition that contemporary antidoctrinalism is just as much the product of social processes as was past attachment to particular churches and their doctrines. Further, the privatism and subjectivism that accompanies the neglect of communal doctrines leads to a weakening of the social groups *(Gemeinschaften)* that are the chief bulwarks against chaos and against totalitarian efforts to master chaos. One can argue, in other words, as did some of the more agnostic founders of the American republic, that an open society needs doctrinally committed religious communities to inculcate the moral and creedal absolutes that are necessary in order to maintain openness. Yet when the *Zeitgeist* is as unfavorable as at present, only a few intellectuals can be expected to be much influenced by such thoughts. Other measures are necessary to convince larger numbers of the importance of doctrine.

It may well be that some measure of what I have on other occasions called "sociological sectarianism" is required.[9] Religious bodies that wish to maintain highly deviant convictions in an inhospitable environment must, it would seem, develop close-knit groups capable of supplying the psychosocial "plausibility structures" (as Peter Berger calls them) needed to sustain an alien faith. These groups need not withdraw into sociological ghettoes in the fashion of the Amish or the Hasidic Jews, but can rather form cells like those of the early Christian movement (or of the more recent international communist one), or develop *ecclesiolae in ecclesia* similar to those of monasticism, early pietism, or some portions of the contemporary charismatic movement.

The overcoming of the current aversion to doctrinal standards and its replacement by concern for correct doctrine depends much more on social and ecclesial developments than on the solution of the theoretical questions with which this book is concerned, yet theory does have a role to play. The conceptual difficulties involved in traditional propositional notions of authoritative teaching have contributed to discrediting the whole doctrinal enterprise. They have helped legitimate unnecessary and counterproductive rigidities in practice because, first, propositionalism makes it difficult to understand how new doctrines can develop in the course of time,[10] and how old ones can be forgotten or become peripheral.[11] Second, propositionalist accounts of how old doctrines can be reinterpreted to fit new circumstances are unconvincing: they have difficulty in distinguishing between what changes and what remains the same.[12] Third, they do not deal adequately with the specifically ecumenical problematic: how is it possible for doctrines that once contradicted each other to be reconciled and yet retain their identity? Experiential-expressivisms that reduce doctrines to nondiscursive symbolisms have an exactly opposite set of difficulties. In each the underlying issue is that of constancy and change, unity and diversity. How can a religion claim to preserve "the faith which was once for all delivered to the saints" (Jude 3), as all religions in some sense do, when it takes so many forms in both the past and the present?

One reaction to these considerations is relativistic. There is no faith once for all delivered to the saints. No self-identical core persists down through the centuries and subsists within the different and usually competing traditions that inevitably develop. Everything is in flux. Christianity (or any other religion for that matter) has only the kind of constancy and unity represented by historical continuities.[13] Such a view is promoted by modern awareness of history and of cultural and individual differences. It has become part of the received wisdom of the educated classes, and attempts to challenge it are often greeted with incredulity.

The contrary extreme is, on the Protestant side, biblicistic, and on the Catholic, traditionalist. The attempt in both cases is to preserve identity by reproducing as literalistically as possible the words and actions of the past.[14] The defect of this tactic is that it confuses the letter and the spirit (as Paul, Augustine, or Luther might have put it). The meaning of rites and utterances depends on contexts. To replicate the old forms in new situations frequently betrays the original meaning, the original spirit. Just as the only way to love parents, spouses, children, and neighbors is to behave toward each in a distinctive fashion, so often the only way to convey the same message is to proclaim it differently. Everyone knows this intuitively, but the fear of relativistic anomie at times leads religious groups to a rigidity that gravely impairs their loyalty to a past they profess to revere.

Doctrine and the theory of doctrine can make only a small contribution to the task of ascertaining which of the changing forms is faithful to the putatively abiding substance.[15] Those who are best able to judge in these matters (as we have already noted in passing and shall see more at length in the discussion of the teaching office) are those who have effectively interiorized a religion. They know by connaturality, as Aquinas might say,[16] whether specific usages are in conformity to the spirit, the interior rule of faith, and do not need the clumsy directives of official dogma. Yet there is also a place for the clumsy directives. Saints and prophets are rare, and doctrinal decisions and reflections on those decisions, while poor substitutes for inspiration, are preferable to uninspired and unreflective prejudice. Thus theoreticians may be of some modest help to religious communities if they can show how doctrines can be both firm and flexible, both abiding and adaptable. To the extent that they are unable to do so, their theories are theologically and pastorally unfruitful.

II
GRAMMAR AND DOCTRINE, CONTINUITY AND CHANGE

The only theories of doctrine that need to be taken seriously for our purposes are regulative and modified propositional ones. Symbolic theories, while perhaps currently the most popular, will be referred to only in passing. As has already been noted, they tend to exclude *a priori* the traditional characteristics of doctrine. The affirmation of the resurrection, for example, cannot easily be an enduring communal norm of belief and practice if it is seen primarily as symbol of a certain type of experience (such as that of the spiritual presence of Christ as the power of the New Being) that can in principle be expressed or evoked in other ways.[17] Similarly, what Lonergan calls "classical" propositional views of doctrine will be disregarded.[18] These tend to take a particular formulation of a doctrine (e.g., a particular description of the resurrection) as a truth claim with objective or ontological import, and thus have difficulty envisioning the possibility of markedly different formulations of the same doctrine. Some modern forms of propositionalism, however, seek to overcome this defect by distinguishing between what a doctrine affirms ontologically and the diverse conceptualities or formulations in which the affirmation can be expressed.[19] They thus allow for the possibility that doctrines have both unchanging and changing aspects. So also, as we shall now see, does a regulative or rule theory, although its analysis of the two aspects is in part very different.

One possible source of confusion needs to be clarified: To say that doctrines are rules is not to deny that they involve propositions. The rules formulated by the linguist or the logician, for example, express propositional convictions about how language or thought actually work. These are, however, second-order rather than first-order propositions and affirm nothing about extra-linguistic or extra-human reality. For a rule theory, in short, doctrines qua doctrines are not first-order propositions, but are to to be construed as second-order ones: they make, as was said in the final section of the previous chapter, intrasystematic rather than ontological truth claims.

It should be recalled in this connection that we are speaking, as was just indicated, of doctrines qua doctrines. This restriction is important because a doctrinal sentence may also function symbolically or as a first-order proposition. Insofar as it is employed in these other ways, as was noted earlier,[20] it either cannot or need not be construed as a norm of communal belief or practice: it is not being used as a church doctrine.

The novelty of rule theory, we must next observe, is that it does not locate the abiding and doctrinally significant aspect of religion in propositionally formulated truths, much less in inner experiences, but in the story it tells and in the grammar that informs the way the story is told and used. From a cultural-linguistic perspective, it will be recalled, a religion is first of all a comprehensive interpretive medium or categorial framework within which one has certain kinds of experiences and makes certain kinds of affirmations. In the case of Christianity, the framework is supplied by the biblical narratives interrelated in certain specified ways (e.g., by Christ as center). Given the linguistic analogy, one can distinguish between vocabulary and grammar. The vocabulary of symbols, concepts, rites, injunctions, and stories is in part highly variable, even though there is a relatively fixed core of lexical elements that correspond roughly, one might say, to basic English. This lexical core is found for the most part in the canonical Scriptures, though by no means everything in the Bible is included (as differences of emphasis on various parts of the Bible testify). Some contributions to the basic vocabulary (e.g., Trinitarian language) may also be made by postbiblical traditions; although this is a point that Catholics and Protestants often interpret differently. In any case, it is not the lexicon but rather the grammar of the religion which church doctrines chiefly reflect. Some doctrines, such as those delimiting the canon and specifying the relation of Scripture and tradition, help determine the vocabulary; while others (or sometimes the same ones) instantiate syntactical rules that guide the use of this material in construing the world, community, and self, and still others provide semantic reference. The doctrine that Jesus is the Messiah, for example, functions lexically as the warrant for adding the New Testament literature to the canon, syntactically as a hermeneutical rule that Jesus Christ be interpreted as the fulfillment of the Old Testament promises (and the Old Testament as pointing toward him), and semantically as a rule regarding the referring use of such titles as "Messiah."

On this view, doctrines acquire their force from their relation to the grammar of a religion. The particular usages they condemn or recommend seem trivial at times, rather like the preference for "am not" rather than "ain't," or for "Chinese" rather than "Chink," but as we have already noted, their triviality may on occasion be only apparent. On one level, for example, nothing depends on whether Christians celebrate the Sabbath on Saturday or Sunday, but in some circumstances it could be of crucial importance. Some doctrines, such as the *sola gratia* or the *sola fide* in Christianity, are explicit statements of general regulative principles, but most doctrines illustrate correct usage rather than define it. They are exemplary instantiations or paradigms of the application of rules. Faithfulness to such doctrines does not necessarily mean repeating them; rather, it requires, in the making of any new formulations, adherence to the same directives that were involved in their first formulation. It is thus—as I shall later argue—that faithfulness to an ancient creed such as the Nicene should be construed. Similarly, to take an example from Latin grammar, *"amo, amas, amat"* operates as a paradigm when one says, e.g., *"rogo, rogas, rogat,"* not when one insists on parroting the original.

Even more than the grammar in grammar books, church doctrine is an inevitably imperfect and often misleading guide to the fundamental interconnections within a religion. In part this is because every formulated rule has more exceptions than the grammarians and the theologians are aware of. Some rules may reflect temporary features of surface grammar or may even be arbitrary impositions (as in the days when attempts were made to force Latin patterns on modern languages). The deep grammar of the language may escape detection. It may be impossible to find rules that show why some crucial usages are beautifully right and other dangerously wrong. The experts must on occasion bow to the superior wisdom of the competent speaker who simply knows that such and such is right or wrong even though it violates the rules they have formulated.[21] Yet, despite these inadequacies, the guidance offered by the grammar or the doctrine of the textbooks may be indispensable, especially to those who are learning a language, to those who have not mastered it well, or to those who, for whatever reason, are in danger of corrupting it into meaninglessness.

It would be both tedious and unprofitable to continue this account of the ways in which grammar and doctrine can be compared. What we need next to observe is how, on this model, the cognitional and experiential dimensions of a religion are variable in contrast to the doctrinally significant grammatical core.

The first-order truth claims of a religion change insofar as these arise from the application of the interpretive scheme to the shifting worlds that human beings inhabit. What is taken to be reality is in large part socially constructed and consequently alters in the course of time. The universe of the ancient Near East was very different from that of Greek philosophy, and both are dissimilar from the modern cosmos. Inevitably, the Christianized versions of these various world pictures are far from identical. When different worlds with their distinct definitions of the good and the real, the divine and the human, are redescribed within one and the same framework of biblical narratives, they continue to remain different worlds. In one world, for example, the origin of things is pictured in terms of a Babylonian myth; in another, in terms of Plato's Timaeus tale; and in a third, in terms of a scientific account of cosmic evolution. The descriptions of God as originator change correspondingly. In the terminology of Aquinas which we earlier utilized, it is at most the *significatum* not the *modus significandi* which remains the same.[22]

This way of putting the matter, it will be noticed, shifts the emphasis from the usual one. It need not be the religion that is primarily reinterpreted as world views change, but rather the reverse: changing world views may be reinterpreted by one and same religion. To be sure, adjustments also take place in the interpretive scheme. We have already mentioned changes in the theoretical or theological, (even if not the ordinary-language) concepts of creator or originator, and the same thing happens in Christology. Jesus Christ, for instance, is in one setting affirmed primarily as the Messiah; in another as the incarnate Logos; and in a third, perhaps, as Bonhoeffer's "Man for Others" or Barth's "Humanity of God." Yet amid these shifts in

Christological affirmations and in the corresponding experiences of Jesus Christ, the story of passion and resurrection and the basic rules for its use remain the same. Theological and religious transformations that lead to relativistic denials of an abiding identity (when one assumes constancy must be propositional, or symbolic, or experiential) can be seen, if one adopts rule theory, as the fusion of a self-identical story with the new worlds within which it is told and retold.

There is nothing uniquely Christian about this constancy: supernatural explanations are quite unnecessary. This is simply the kind of stability that languages and religions, and to a lesser extent cultures, observably have. They are the lenses[23] through which human beings see and respond to their changing worlds, or the media in which they formulate their descriptions. The world and its descriptions may vary enormously even while the lenses or media remain the same. Or, to change the simile, just as genetic codes or computer programs may remain identical even while producing startling different products depending on input and situation, so also with the basic grammars of cultures, languages, and religions. They remain while the products change.

The experiences generated by a religion are on this view just as variable as its propositionally stable descriptions of the world and of God. This contrasts with an expressivist model, which locates what is religiously normative and abiding in the depths of the inner self. Such a model may suggest that the experience of love, for example, identifies what is truly Christian, but for rule theory, it is the Christian story which alone is able to identify what for Christians is true love. The experience of love, conditioned as it is by psychic and cultural factors, may vary, but insofar as it is authentically shaped by the story of Jesus it qualifies as Christian. The experience in itself is a variable because it is a function of the interaction of changing selves in changing circumstances with the selfsame story.

It may be that the sentiments, feelings, moods, and emotions characteristic of Christian love have been in some sense basically the same down through the centuries, but the evidence of hymns and art forms makes this seem implausible. To be sure, the agonies of Grünewald's *Crucifixion* are unimaginable as an image of goodness on Buddhist soil; and Christians, on their side, could never make central the inward-looking contemplative serenity embodied in statues of Gautama. One can, in other words, distinguish to some extent characteristically Buddhist and characteristically Christian feelings and attitudes. Leaving aside such extreme cases, however, the range between Grünewald's Christ and a Byzantine Pantocrator is so immense that it seems impossible phenomenologically to identify a common experiential core. In any case, in the cultural-linguistic approach, there is no urge to do so. It is their common object rather than some commonality of feeling tone which gives different forms of love whatever specifically Christian distinctiveness they may have. What is important is that Christians allow their cultural conditions and highly diverse affections to be molded by the set of biblical stories that stretches from creation to eschaton and culminates in Jesus' passion and resurrection. The experiential products of this shaping process, however, will be endlessly varied because of the differences of the affective materials on which it works.

Thus, in the approach we are considering, changes in inner experience, like those in affirmation, are not opposed to continuity. They are rather marks of vitality. It is only in dead or imperfectly known languages and religions that no new words are used, truths uttered, or feelings expressed. Nor need this variety impair identity. One and the same language can be spoken on Florida beaches and Arctic tundra, and one and the same religion practiced in Constantinople and the catacombs, even though the affirmations that are made and the feelings that are experienced may be fantastically different.

From this perspective, the difficulty with locating the constant element in a religion on the level of either objective description or inner experience is that this tends to result in the identification of the normative form of the religion with either the truth claims or the experiences appropriate to a particular world, whether that of Constantinople or the catacombs, of Florida or the Arctic. Then to be a Christian one must think, perhaps, like a medieval scholastic or a contemporary liberationist, or have an existential stance like that of Jesus. It may be more difficult to grasp the notion that it is the framework and the medium within which Christians know and experience, rather than what they experience or think they know, that retains continuity and unity down through the centuries. Yet this seems to make more empirical, historical, and doctrinal sense. To the degree that religions are like languages, they can obviously remain the same amid vast transformations of affirmation and experience. When put this way, it seems almost self-evident that the permanence and unity of doctrines, despite changing and diverse formulation, is more easily accounted for if they are taken to resemble grammatical rules rather than propositions or expressive symbols (though, as we have noted, the same sentences in which the rules are stated may function in these other ways also).

III
A TAXONOMY OF DOCTRINES

These general considerations have been simply preliminary to the question of whether doctrines do in fact allow themselves to be understood as comparable to rules. This is the theme of the present section. We shall have occasion to make frequent comparisons with propositional interpretations because these, unlike symbolic views of doctrine, do admit the possibility affirmed in most religious traditions that doctrines may legitimately function as norms of belief and practice.

The disagreement centers on beliefs about what is ontologically true, rather than on practical doctrines (which are by definition rules rather than truth claims). This makes it desirable to start with practical doctrines in considering the various ways in which rules can be permanently valid before we move on to the more problematic question of whether doctrines that concern beliefs can also be satisfactorily understood as regulative.

Some practical doctrines, such as the "law of love" in Christianity, are held to be unconditionally necessary. They are part of the indispensable grammar or logic of the faith. There are, for example, no circumstances in which Christians are commanded not to love God or neighbor. Other rules, however, are conditionally essential. This is the way most churches now interpret the prohibition against Christian participation in war. It applied in the early days of the church, it may be mandatory for individual pacifists with a special vocation, and it perhaps is or will once again become communally mandatory in the nuclear age; but under the circumstances prevailing during most of Christian history, pacifism has not generally been regarded as obligatory. It is not, so most churches hold, an unconditionally necessary consequence of the Christian rule of love, though it may be conditionally necessary.

While all unconditionally essential doctrines are permanent, the conditional variety may be either permanent or temporary. If the relevant conditions always obtain, the doctrinal rule remains operative as long as the religion endures, even though it is conditional. "Feed the poor," for example, is a permanent even if conditional injunction if it is in fact true that "the poor you will always have with you." Most of the current debates in the realm of sexual ethics can be analyzed as arguments over whether the conditions under which certain traditional moral doctrines apply are permanent or have been abrogated by developments in science, technology, society, and culture.

Temporarily conditional doctrines can, in turn, be subdivided into the reversible and irreversible ones. The views of war that have already been mentioned may serve as illustrations of the first, reversible kind. If, on the other hand, some historical changes are irreversible, then the doctrines occasioned by these changes are themselves irreversible. The condemnation of slavery, which now has at least informal doctrinal status in all the major Christian traditions, would seem to be an example. Christians at first shared the consensus of classical cultures that slavery was an inescapable institution (although they differed from many others in thinking of it as unnatural, a result of sin). Once historical developments taught them, however, that societies without institutionalized chattel slavery are possible, they came to think, despite the absence of scriptural commands, that the logic of the biblical story demands not only humane treatment of slaves but struggle against the institution itself. Assuming that history is sufficiently cumulative so that awareness of the possibility of slaveless societies will not disappear, the Christian obligation to oppose slavery is irreversible even though conditional.

A final possibility is that a doctrine may be neither unconditionally nor conditionally, but simply accidentally necessary. In some cases, a given practice could just as well have been otherwise, but once established, it becomes pointless or impossibly difficult to change it. The decision to drive on the right rather than the left side of the road may in our society be such an accidental but quite possibly permanent rule. Except for the fact that it has become the standard procedure, this rule could just as well be otherwise even now; and yet it is so deeply interwoven in the fabric of our lives that, apart from massive pressures to change (such as the British now confront because they drive on the left while most of the rest of the world drives on the right), it is best for the welfare of the people that it remain unchanged. Postbiblical liturgical developments such as Sunday and Christmas celebrations might serve as examples; but, more controversially, some Protestant theologians appear to grant the possibility that even the papacy may have this kind of accidental and possibly permanent (though in principle reversible) normativeness. Roman Catholic theologians, in contrast, generally hold that though the understanding and practice of papal primacy may alter, a universal teaching office in the church institutionally continuous in some fashion with the papacy is an irreversible development.[24] In any case, the purpose of a classificatory scheme such as this is not to settle material questions about the nature or location of particular doctrines, but rather to indicate the formal possibilities and thereby to enhance the chances of meaningful discussion and debate.

Now if doctrines that propose beliefs are treated as rules, the same scheme can be applied to them. They also can be viewed as unconditionally or conditionally necessary, as permanent or temporary, as reversible or irreversible. Historically, for example, the articles of the Apostles' Creed and the ancient Trinitarian and Christological confessions of faith of Nicaea and Chalcedon have been treated as unconditionally and permanently essential. A doctrine such as the immortality of the soul, in contrast, could perhaps be classified as conditional, temporary, and reversible. It could be argued that this belief is necessary to the integrity of Christian faith only when believers think in terms of a classical mind-body dualism, but not when their anthropology is Hebraic or modern.[25] A third group of beliefs, such as the Marian ones, have traditionally been viewed by Roman Catholics as conditionally necessary (for they were not always considered essential, and were even widely rejected), but yet irreversible. Whether anyone would think that there are legitimate doctrinal beliefs (in contrast to practices) which are "accidentally" necessary seems to me doubtful. At least, I fail to think of plausible examples.

One possible objection to this notion of temporary and reversible doctrines does not seem to hold. It does not in any direct way contradict the official Roman Catholic view that all church doctrines are permanent. A temporary actual necessity may be a permanent conditional one. It may—as has already been suggested—be permanently necessary for Christians to affirm the immortality of the soul whenever they think in terms of a classical soul-body dualism, but not when their anthropology is Hebraic or modern. Whatever one may think of this particular example, it illustrates the logical possibility of conditionally permanent doctrines. Whenever such and such a condition prevails, such and such a doctrine applies. It is thus the condition, not the doctrine, which is temporary or "reformable." While the bishops at Vatican I never envisioned the possibility of "permanently conditional" doctrines, and therefore neither accepted nor rejected them, there seems to be no reason why such doctrines cannot be called *irreformabiles* in the full sense of the conciliar definition (DS 3074). That definition apparently need not create difficulties at this point for a rule theory.

We must also ask, however, whether the beliefs earlier mentioned can be plausibly classified as done here. The articles of the Apostles' Creed and the doctrine of immortality raise the fewest questions. The Apostolicum is, in effect, largely lexical: it certifies the indispensability of central elements in the biblical story of God as Father, Son, and Holy Spirit, and therefore has been easily accepted as unconditionally necessary. Immortality in the technical sense is equally clearly a postbiblical import from Greek philosophy, and therefore a good candidate for conditionality.

Problems arise, however, in reference to the classical Trinitarian and Christological doctrines of Nicaea and Chalcedon, on the one hand, and the Marian dogmas, on the other. The major traditions have historically held that the first are unconditionally permanent, a restatement of essential scriptural teaching in new language, but it has also been widely argued, not least in modern times, that they are conditional and perhaps reversible (not to mention the extreme view that even at the time of their formulation they were simply illegitimate, simply a mistake). The argument over the Marian dogmas, among those who accept their legitimacy, is rather different. They are, in their church doctrinal form, obviously conditional (for they were not in existence through much of church history). The question is whether rule theory allows (but does not require) them to be understood as irreversible.

Lastly, claims of infallibility also need to be looked at. These raise questions of a logically distinct order that concern, not the nature of church doctrines *in se,* but the kind of certainty that can legitimately be ascribed to them by the religious communities in which they are affirmed. Yet this epistemological dimension must also be taken into consideration in an examination of the confessional neutrality and potential ecumenical usefulness of construing doctrines as rules. The next chapter, therefore, tests the theory by brief discussions of the meaningfulness (as distinct from the correctness) of attributing unconditionality to classic Christological and Trinitarian affirmations, irreversibility to Marian developments, and infallibility to *de fide* pronouncements.

NOTES

1. The large literature on the meaning of "doctrine," "dogma," "creed," "confession," and related terms generally agrees with the "noncontroversial" features that I have listed below, but it is written from perspectives other than the "cultural-linguistic" one which we are exploring, and cannot, therefore, be cited in direct support. Jaroslav Pelikan's characterization of Christian doctrine as "what the church of Jesus Christ believes, teaches, and confesses on the basis of the word of God" (*The Christian Tradition: A History of the Development of Doctrine,* Vol. 1 [University of Chicago Press, 1971], p. 1) does not distinguish as sharply between church doctrine and theology as the purposes of the present essay make desirable. Bernard Lonergan, in contrast, draws the line between church doctrines and theological and methodological ones at much the same point that I do (*Method in Theology* [Herder & Herder, 1972], pp. 296f.). For an earlier version of the understanding of doctrine here presented, see George A. Lindbeck, "Creed and Confession," *Encyclopaedia Britannica,* 15th ed. (1974), Macropaedia 5, pp. 243–246.

2. Martin Luther, *WA-BR,* Vol. 3, pp. 81f.

3. Cited by Garry Wills, *Bare Ruined Choirs* (Doubleday & Co., 1972), pp. 64–65.

4. Edward Gibbon, *The History of the Decline and Fall of the Roman Empire,* ed. by J. B. Bury (London, 1896–1900), Vol. 2, p. 352.

5. Hans Küng, at least in his book on *Justification: The Doctrine of Karl Barth and a Catholic Reflection* (Thomas Nelson & Sons, 1964; Westminster Press, 1981), may serve as an example of a Roman Catholic "Barthian," while much of Anglican theology from the time of Jeremy Taylor (d. 1667) has been self-consciously "Erasmian."

6. See "Was ist eine dogmatische Aussage?" by Karl Rahner, published separately in *Catholica* 15 (1961), pp. 161–184; and the companion essay by Wolfhart Pannenberg in *Kerygma und Dogma* 8 (1962), pp. 81–99. For the history of the meaning of the word "dogma," see Karl Rahner and Karl Lehmann, "Kerygma und

Dogma," in J. Feiner and M. Loehrer (eds.), *Mysterium Salutis* (Einsiedeln: Benzinger, 1965), pp. 622–703, esp. 639–661.

7. This paragraph rehearses from a somewhat different perspective comments already made in Chapter 1, section II, above.

8. Gregory Baum, *Faith and Doctrine, A Contemporary View* (Paulist Press, 1969), is a Roman Catholic example; but Baum, as could be expected of a theologian, does not draw the popular consequences listed here.

9. For the argument of this paragraph, see my articles cited in Chapter 1, n. 22, above. I return to this theme in the last section of the last chapter.

10. The resistance of both Protestants and Catholics to the notion of development in doctrine is well described by Owen Chadwick, *From Bossuet to Newman: The Idea of Doctrinal Development* (Cambridge: Cambridge University Press, 1957).

11. For the notion of a forgotten doctrine, see Karl Rahner, "Forgotten Truths Regarding the Sacrament of Penance," *Theological Investigations,* Vol. 2 (Helicon Press, 1963), pp. 155–170.

12. Contemporary Roman Catholic controversies over the many proposed (and often radical) reinterpretations of almost every conceivable dogma have been sharpest in reference to the eucharistic presence, infallibility, and Christology. The last topic is also much discussed in non-Roman Catholic circles, but Anglican and mainline Protestant communions have for the most part abandoned the attempt to draw explicit doctrinal lines. See, e.g., *Christian Believing: The Nature of the Christian Faith and Its Expression in Holy Scripture and Creeds: A Report of the Doctrinal Commission of the Church of England* (London: S.P.C.K., 1976).

13. This has been argued at length by Wilfred Cantwell Smith, *The Meaning and End of Religion: A New Approach to the Religious Traditions of Mankind* (Macmillan Co., 1963).

14. What I have in mind here is popular attitudes. No theologian who is at all well informed and intellectually responsible, no matter how conservative, not even a J. Gresham Machen or a Cardinal Ottaviani, denies the need for some kinds of change.

15. "The substance of the ancient doctrine of the deposit of faith is one thing, and the way in which it is presented is another." (John XXIII; *The Documents of Vatican II,* ed. by W. M. Abbott [Herder & Herder, 1966], p. 715.) This distinction between the "form" and "substance" of doctrines was used by John XXIII in his opening speech to the Second Vatican Council.

16. See Chapter 2, n. 12, above.

17. Paul Tillich, *Systematic Theology,* Vol. 2 (University of Chicago Press, 1957), pp. 154–158, esp. 157. Tillich says that the "picture of Jesus of Nazareth becomes indissolubly united with the reality of the New Being," but does not in this place affirm the converse relation. For a fuller discussion of Tillich's view of the finality of Christ, see George Lindbeck, "An Assessment Re-assessed: Paul Tillich on the Reformation," *Journal of Religion* 63/4 (1983), pp. 376–393, esp. 391f.

18. Bernard Lonergan, *Doctrinal Pluralism* (Marquette University Press, 1971).

19. This procedure is not confined to Roman Catholics such as Rahner and

Lonergan. For an ecumenically seminal discussion from the Protestant side, see Edmund Schlink, "The Structure of Dogmatic Statements as an Ecumenical Problem," *The Coming Christ and the Coming Church* (Fortress Press, 1968), pp. 16–84.

20. See Chapter 1, section I, above.

21. The notion of appealing to the "intuitions" of those who are linguistically "competent" is derived from Chomsky, but I am using the terms, not in the full technical sense of Chomsky's theories, but with the more general meaning described, e.g., by John Lyons, *Noam Chomsky* (Viking Press, 1970), pp. 38–39, 96–97.

22. In a cognitivist approach, one might say that the propositional substance (e.g., *creatio ex nihilo*) is unaltered while the conceptual form changes; but if the analysis in Chapter 3, section IV (above), is adopted, all efforts to isolate the "substance" *(significatum)*—including "God creates out of nothing"—from the *modi significandi* are bound to fail. The affirmation that God creates *ex nihilo* can serve as a guide to the way believers should speak and act, but whether it has propositional force depends (as does the more mythological language of Genesis) on the "ordinary language" context in which it is uttered.

23. The metaphor of lenses or "spectacles" was employed by Calvin (though with specific reference to Scripture). See *Institutes* I.6.1.

24. George Lindbeck, "Papacy and *ius divinum:* A Lutheran View," in Paul C. Empie et al. (eds.), *Papal Primacy and the Universal Church* (Augsburg Publishing House, 1974), pp. 193–207.

25. This is the line taken by H. Engelland, *Evangelisches Kirchenlexikon* Vol. 3 (Göttingen: Vandenhoeck & Ruprecht, 1962), cols. 1579f. J. Splett, in contrast, argues that the substance of the doctrine of immortality can be retained even though it must now be given a very different (post-Kantian) conceptual form by being grounded on the "immanent basic experience of freedom itself [which] experiences itself in the experience of the unconditional claim of truth and of good." (*Encyclopedia of Theology,* ed. by Karl Rahner [Seabury Press, 1975], p. 689.)

CHAPTER 5

TESTING THE THEORY: CHRISTOLOGY, MARIOLOGY, AND INFALLIBILITY

The purpose of this chapter is to test the theological and ecumenical usefulness of a rule theory of doctrine (and, by implication, of the cultural-linguistic understanding of religion associated with it) by seeing whether it works in the hard cases: in reference to claims of the unconditionality of classic Christological (and Trinitarian) affirmations, the irreversibility of Marian developments, and the infallibility of the teaching office. These claims are the topics of the first three sections of this chapter. Can the theory make sense of these doctrines and yet not decide the substantive issue of whether they should be accepted? Can it give some nonvacuous meaning to unconditionality, irreversibility, and infallibility while still leaving open the question of whether these predicates are rightly assigned? If it can, the theory is successful: it provides a nonreductive framework for discussion among those who genuinely disagree.

The debate in this chapter, as in the last section of Chapter 3, is basically between regulative and propositional perspectives on doctrine. Purely expressive-symbolic interpretations can be disregarded because (as we have noted and shall note again) they make meaningless the historic doctrinal affirmations of unconditionality, irreversibility, or infallibility, and thus leave nothing to discuss. In the fourth and concluding section, therefore, I shall briefly compare regulative and propositional approaches and suggest that the former has advantages, not only because it can give a more plausible account, than can the alternatives, of the permanence of doctrine amid historical change, but also for the traditional and yet modern-sounding reason that it makes church doctrines more effectively normative by relating them more closely to praxis. This contention is not necessary to the main thesis of this book (which is concerned simply with the availability, not the superiority, of a rule theory of doctrine and the associated cultural-linguistic view of religion), but it does seem to be a conclusion implied by the total argument.

I
NICAEA AND CHALCEDON

In order to argue successfully for the unconditionality and permanence of the ancient Trinitarian and Christological creeds, it is necessary to make a distinction between doctrines, on the one hand, and the terminology and conceptuality in which they are formulated, on the other. As was noted in the previous chapter, this is a point that is recognized by propositionalists and is not dependent on adopting a regulative or symbolic-expressive view of doctrine. Some of the crucial concepts employed by these creeds, such as "substance" *(ousia),* "person" *(hypostasis),* and "in two natures" *(en dyo physeis),* are postbiblical novelties. If these particular notions are essential, the doctrines of these creeds are clearly conditional, dependent on the late-Hellenistic milieu. Furthermore, their irreversibility would then seem to be dependent on the irreversibility of the conditioning circumstances, that is, on Greek philosophy. This, at any rate, is the way in which opponents have argued, beginning in the fourth century, but even more in modern times.[1] The argument—to repeat—is compelling unless a distinction can be made between doctrine and formulation, between content and form.

Whatever may be true in other religions, such a distinction seems to be required in Christianity. It seems that from the very beginning this religion has been committed to the possibility of expressing the same faith, the same teaching, and the same doctrine in diverse ways. This is illustrated by the multiplicity of Christological titles in the New Testament. No particular words or specific interpretive notions are uniquely sacrosanct. The fundamental conviction about the central importance of Jesus was expressed in terms of both *christos* and *kyrios,* both Messiahship and Lordship, to Hebrew- and Greek-reading audiences respectively. Because their sacred scriptures were produced over many centuries by a wide variety of authors, Christians are under unusual pressure to be nonliteralistic (in the sense of somehow differentiating between form and content) in order to maintain the unity of the canon.

Unless one adopts either a propositional or a regulative interpretation, it is difficult to make this differentiation while at the same time preserving the distinctiveness of a given doctrine (or religion). On a symbolic view where doctrines are equated with the images in which they are expressed, a distinction between form and content is, so to speak, not within doctrines but between doctrines and experience. When the form of nondiscursive symbolism, whether in art or religion, is altered, so generally is the experience it communicates or expresses. It is not surprising, therefore, that many of those who at present most vigorously attack the classical doctrine of the incarnation in fact identify it with the picture (or, as they generally put it, "the myth") of God descending and taking on human flesh. They sometimes object to the hierarchical and authoritarian attitudes which they think this myth evokes and reinforces. One reply to this objection is that context also helps determine the evocative import of a symbol. The myth of the incarnation may function in some cultural or psychological settings to strengthen the self-respect of the downtrodden and oppressed, rather than, as happens in other contexts, to legitimate the condescension of superiors.[2] Nevertheless, the original problem remains: it is quite true that form, when taken in conjunction with context, is inseparable from content (i.e., experience) in the case of nondiscursive symbols, with the result that when the form or context alters, so does the content or substance of the symbol (or of the doctrine insofar as it is construed as a symbol). Thus, to provide a further illustration, those who argue that calling God "he" or "she" changes the very substance of the doctrine are quite right from some experiential-expressive perspectives.

In contrast to this, it is self-evident that both first-order and second-order propositions (e.g., rules) are separable from the forms in which they are articulated. One and the same proposition can be expressed in a variety of sentences employing a variety of conceptualities. The fact that so-and-so has jaundice can be affirmed in the idiom of Galen's medical theories (an imbalance of the humors) or that of modern science (a viral infection). The fact that the sun strikes the observatory in Greenwich at 6 A.M. on the vernal or autumnal equinox can be stated in the language of either the sun rising or the earth revolving. Similarly, one and the same grammatical structure or operation can be described and redescribed in different ways without altering the regulative import. One conceptuality may be scientifically more satisfactory than the other, but the change in conceptuality need not change the truth claim or rule that is being enunciated.

Yet while the same content can be expressed in different formulations, there is no way of stating independently what that content is. For example, "12" in base four is equal to "6" in base ten, but there is no device for specifying the common number apart from mathematical notation. One can grasp the self-identical content as distinct from the form only by seeing that the diverse formulations are equivalent and, usually in a second step, by stating the equivalency rules. Similarly, the only way to show that the doctrines of Nicaea and Chalcedon are distinguishable from the concepts in which they are formulated is to state these doctrines in different terms that nevertheless have equivalent consequences.

This is easier to do if the doctrines are taken as expressing second-order guidelines for Christian discourse rather than first-order affirmations about the inner being of God or of Jesus Christ. That they can be understood as second-order propositions (i.e., rules) is an ancient insight.[3] In his extensive studies of the development of the Trinitarian and Christological dogmas,[4] Lonergan, for one, persuasively argues that these are the product of systematic reflection on the confused multiplicity of presystematic symbols, titles, and predicates applied to God and Jesus Christ. The Christians learned from the Greeks the technique of operating on propositions, of formulating propositions about propositions. As a result of this "logical" (or one could also say "grammatical") analysis of the data of Scripture and tradition, Athanasius expressed the meaning of, for example, consubstantiality in terms of the rule that whatever is said of the Father is said of the Son, except that the Son is not the Father *(eadem de Filio quae de Patre dicuntur excepto Patris Nomine).* [5] Thus the theologian most responsible for the final triumph of Nicaea thought of it, not as a first-order proposition with ontological reference, but as a second-order rule of speech. For him, to accept the doctrine meant to agree to speak in a certain way. He and other early fathers did not deny first-order interpretations, but according to Lonergan, these were at first only "incipient."[6] It was only later, in medieval scholasticism, that the full metaphysical import of the doctrine was asserted[7] (but whether this was, as Lonergan assumes, a desirable development is, as we shall later see, a debatable question).

It is beyond the scope of this essay to examine the historical evidence for a regulative rather than propositional interpretation of the origins of the ancient creeds, but it is easy (indeed, banal) to illustrate what such an interpretation might look like. Three regulative principles[8] at least were obviously at work. First, there is the monotheistic principle: there is only one God, the God of Abraham, Isaac, Jacob, and Jesus. Second, there is the principle of historical specificity: the stories of Jesus refer to a genuine human being who was born, lived, and died in a particular time and place. Third, there is the principle of what may be infelicitously called Christological maximalism: every possible importance is to be ascribed to Jesus that is not inconsistent with the first rules. This last rule, it may be noted, follows from the central Christian conviction that Jesus Christ is the highest possible clue (though an often dim and ambiguous one to creaturely and sinful eyes) within the space-time world of human experience to God, i.e., to what is of maximal importance.

Only the first of these rules was formulated in the early church in something like the terminology I have used, but all three were clearly at work even in the New Testament period. It would not be difficult to analyze four centuries of Trinitarian and Christological development as the product of the joint logical pressure of these three principles constraining Christians to use available conceptual and symbolic materials to relate Jesus Christ to God in certain ways and not in others. Docetism, Gnosticism, Adoptionism, Sabellianism, Arianism, Nestorianism, and Monophysitism were each rejected because they were felt in the concrete life and worship of the Christian community to violate the limits of what was acceptable as defined by the interaction of these three criteria. With the possible exception of Arianism,[9] it seems almost self-evident that what ultimately became Catholic orthodoxy was a cognitively less dissonant adjustment to the joint pressure of these three rules than any of the rejected heresies. It can thus be argued that the Nicene and Chalcedonian formulations were among the few, and perhaps the only, possible outcomes of the process of adjusting Christian discourse to the world of late classical antiquity in a manner conformable to regulative principles that were already at work in the earliest strata of the tradition. These creeds can be understood by Christian and non-Christian alike as paradigmatically instantiating doctrinal rules that have been abidingly important from the beginning in forming mainstream Christian identity.[10]

Paradigms, it will be recalled, are not simply to be replicated, but are rather to be followed in the making of new formulations. The terminology and concepts of "one substance and three persons" or "two natures" may be absent, but if the same rules that guided the formation of the original paradigms are operative in the construction of the new formulations, they express one and the same doctrine. There may, on this reading, be complete faithfulness to classical Trinitarianism and Christology even when the imagery and language of Nicaea and Chalcedon have disappeared from the theology and ordinary worship, preaching, and devotion.

This does not necessarily mean, however, that the creeds should be rewritten to fit the new situation. For one thing, doctrinal paradigms accepted by the church as a whole are rare and difficult achievements. Further, the Nicene Creed in particular has acquired liturgical and expressive functions that are in some respects more important than its doctrinal use for large parts of Christendom. The act of reciting it is for millions a mighty symbol of the church's unity in space and time. Lastly, and rather oddly, archaic and even unintelligible conceptuality may in some ways be better fitted for the statement of general rules than is language alive with contemporary meaning. Unfamiliar concepts can more easily be treated as replaceable. They function as "x's," blanks, or open variables to be filled by whatever symbolic or intellectual content is most effective in a given setting. An updated version of the creed, in contrast, is less likely to invite believers to worship, proclaim, and confess the faith in their language rather than its own.

Yet, though the ancient formulations may have continuing value, they do not on the basis of rule theory have doctrinal authority. That authority belongs rather to the rules they instantiate. If these rules, as was earlier suggested, are such regulative principles as monotheism, historical specificity, and Christological maximalism, it is at least plausible to claim that Nicaea and Chalcedon represent historically conditioned formulations of doctrines that are unconditionally and permanently necessary to mainstream Christian identity. Rule theory, in short, allows (though it does not require) giving these creeds the status that the major Christian traditions have attributed to them, but with the understanding that they are permanently authoritative paradigms, not formulas to be slavishly repeated.

II
MARIAN DOGMAS

Marian beliefs such as the Immaculate Conception and the Assumption represent another kind of problem. Two of the ways in which they differ from the doctrines we have so far considered are particularly important for our purposes. First, as Lonergan among others notes,[11] they are much more the products of developments in cult and sensibility and much less the results of systematic reflection than either the putatively unconditional Trinitarian and Christological affirmations or (it can be added) such apparently conditional doctrines as that of the soul's immortality. Second, their adherents have nevertheless generally regarded them as irreversible. From their point of view, they represent new but enduringly valid discoveries or insights into what was previously only implicit in Christian faith. The question we ask is how rule theory might explain the possibility of such irreversibility in postbiblical developments of this particular kind.

The question, it should be recalled, is formal and not material. We are asking whether a regulative approach leaves the theological options open and is therefore capable of accommodating irreversibility as well as reversibility (not to mention the usual Protestant view, which the rule theory also allows, that these doctrines are simply illegitimate).

The case for both irreversibility and reversibility can be most easily discussed in reference to the Immaculate Conception, although a similar pattern of argument could also be developed for the Assumption.[12] In favor of the possibility of irreversibility, it could be pointed out that every idiom has hidden constraints on what can and cannot be said within it. Sometimes quite new discoveries are made as to what these are (as, for example, Gödel's theorem). In religion no less than in mathematics or natural languages, the exploration of the constraints is a never-ending task. One finds out what they are only by trying to say new things and either failing or succeeding. This was what happened in the varied and often aberrant developments of Marian piety. Only after a new consensus on Mary had developed did it become possible to identify the constraining and enabling grammatical or logical principles. It was only then that precisely the right question could be posed in precisely the right way so that it became revelatory of the underlying structure. It was only after the long, slow growth of Marian devotion, combined with an Augustinian doctrine of original sin and a keen awareness of God's respect for the freedom of his creatures, that the question of the Immaculate Conception could be properly raised or answered. It was answered positively because Christian sensibilities rebelled against attributing sin to Mary even in the first moment of her life. Their abhorrence of this notion was justified because on the level of lived piety, even if this is not provable by theological speculation, it is incompatible with Mary's freedom in becoming *Theotokos* and, more crucially, with God's humility and condescension in waiting on a creaturely "yes" (which, to be sure, he himself graciously provided). Thus Christians discovered that the grammar of their faith required them to speak of the Mother of our Lord as sinless in a way concealed from the first generations.

It is almost self-evident, however, that the same doctrine can also be interpreted as reversible. One can say, for example, that it is only in the context of a questionable Western theology and sense of sin[13] that it is necessary to exempt the Mother of our Lord from all natal stain in order to maintain her God-given and God-dependent freedom in saying "yes" to the angel's terrifying announcement. This is not a denial of the doctrine. As in the case of our earlier and simpler example of the immortality of the soul, one could view the Immaculate Conception as a valid application in particular circumstances of permanently essential rules. The difference is that here, as we have noted, it is much more difficult to specify what the underlying rules might be. One might have to content oneself with saying that they have to do with the uncodifiable aspects of the interaction of divine and human freedom. Furthermore, although the positive affirmation of the Immaculate Conception would be temporary or reversible, it could still be maintained that it is irreformably wrong to assert the negative: that Mary was born in original sin. This, indeed, would be meaningless, because it is the traditional Western notion of original sin which has become problematic. Thus the reason this doctrine, unlike the Trinitarian and Christological ones, can be easily understood as reversible is that some of the rules involved in its emergence (viz., those connected with a particular theology of sin) seem themselves to be temporary.

If this analysis is correct, a rule theory can meet at least the more obvious dogmatic exigencies of the major forms of historic Christianity, including the especially strenuous ones of Roman Catholicism. It allows one to hold that doctrines, whether conditionally or unconditionally essential to the community of faith, are "irreformable," and that even those which are conditional may in some cases be irreversible. Furthermore, it does not settle material questions regarding the status of specific doctrines, and thus leaves room for both doctrinal development and doctrinal "de-development," for both the Catholic openness to the multiplication of dogmas and the Reformation desire to prune back excrescences. Whether the scope of the theory can also allow for the meaningfulness of claims to magisterial infallibility has not yet been tested, however, and to this question we must now turn.

III
INFALLIBILITY

Infallibility is logically distinct from the doctrinal issues we have so far discussed because it has more to do with the nature of the church than with that of doctrine. It is not doctrines but the doctrinal decisions of a community or of teachers within the community which are said to be infallible. Doctrines, in contrast, are not infallible but "irreformable" (though not in the sense that the formulations cannot be changed, but in the sense that they were correct in their original contexts and thus always hold whenever the contexts are in the relevant respects sufficiently similar).[14]

An infallible decision is one that is immune, not from every conceivable defect (for this is true only of God), but from a particular kind of defect. Infallibility, in the view of such a contemporary defender of the doctrine as Karl Rahner, is immunity from ultimately serious error, an error that divides the church definitively from Jesus Christ.[15] Thus in terms of our previous analysis, an infallible church or magisterium would be one that does not make definitive (i.e., dogmatic) mistakes about what beliefs and practices are vitally necessary—or perilous—to the identity or welfare of the community. This does not exclude the possibility that it might sometimes have to make a decision between two alternatives, both of which are bad, but one of which is worse than the other.[16] Its infallibility would then be exercised through its choice of the lesser evil.

A description of this view of infallibility in terms of rule theory involves no special difficulties. Doctrinal definitions are thought of as comparable to grammatical decisions about the correctness or incorrectness of particular usages. They need not involve any grand generalizations about the structure of a religion's language, much less about ontological realities. To affirm infallibility is simply to claim that the church and/or its magisterium does not mortally violate the grammar of the faith in its solemn decisions on particular issues that are essential to the church's identity or welfare.

One advantage of stressing the resemblance of doctrinal to grammatical decisions is that this makes it possible to give the doctrine of infallibility a partly empirical meaning. It suggests explanations, as we shall see, for how the Holy Spirit operates in preserving the church from error. Regulative versions of the doctrine cannot as easily be accused of vacuity as propositional ones. Further, non-Roman Catholic Christians need not entirely dissent from infallibility when it is thus understood (although the attribution by Vatican I of an infallibility not derived from the consent of the church [*non ex consensu ecclesiae*] to papal definitions may be irreconcilable with what they could accept).

In exploring further the empirical meaning that can be given to infallibility on this approach, we shall ask who or what can be appealed to as most nearly infallible in grammatical and, by transference, doctrinal matters. The most obvious answer is what the theological tradition calls the *consensus fidelium* or *consensus ecclesiae*.

Just as the contemporary linguist tests technical grammatical formulations by seeing whether their ordinary-language consequences are acceptable or unacceptable to competent speakers of the language being investigated, so the student of a religion submits the consequences of doctrinal formulations to the judgment of competent practitioners of that religion: "Are they offensive to pious ears?" to quote a familiar adage.

There is, however, a special difficulty in applying this procedure to highly variegated religions such as Christianity. Who are the competent practitioners? Who have the pious ears? Are they Arians or Athanasians, Catholics or Protestants, the masses of conventional churchgoers or an elite of saints or theologians? Competence in natural languages is easy to identify. It is possessed by native speakers and a few nonnative ones who can communicate effectively in a given tongue. The limits of the language are marked by the point at which variations in dialect become so great that communication is impossible apart from learning the idiom as foreign speech. Among Christians, however, there are many groups who seem to speak mutually unintelligible dialects. This has been true not only of marginal sects such as Mormons, Jehovah's Witnesses, or Christian Scientists but also for major groups such as Arians and Athanasians, Latins and Greeks, Catholics and Protestants. Which claimants to the authentic Christian tongue should be heeded?

In trying to answer this question, the nontheological investigator is likely to employ in his or her own fashion tests that are also familiar to the theologians. The investigator will wish to draw a sample from as large a cross section, as wide a consensus, as is possible, and will therefore refer to tradition, to magisterial pronouncements (as voices of the tradition and of consensus), and to the canonical writings as generally accepted instances of genuinely Christian (or Islamic, or Buddhist, or Jewish) speech. These criteria make it possible to delimit a mainstream of the religion in question from which to draw a sample of competent practitioners.

A further test, however, is needed. Membership in a mainstream community does not guarantee competence. Whatever might be true of other religions, especially of culturally homogeneous primitive ones, most Christians through most of Christian history have spoken their own official tongue very poorly. It has not become a native language, the primary medium in which they think, feel, act, and dream. Thus, lacking competence, they cannot, from the cultural-linguistic perspective, be part of that *consensus fidelium* against which doctrinal proposals are tested.

This demand for competence is the empirical equivalent of insisting on the Spirit as one of the tests of doctrine. In cultural-linguistic categories the role of the Spirit can be more easily stressed than in cognitivist ones, and is less subject to enthusiasm or *Schwärmerei* than in an experiential approach. These categories suggest at least partially objective tests for identifying the Spirit-filled. The linguistically competent, to recapitulate, are to be sought in the mainstream, rather than in isolated backwaters or ingrown sects uninterested in communicating widely. They must, in other words, be what in the first centuries was meant by "catholic" or "orthodox," and what we now generally call "ecumenical." Further, the competence that they have must to some extent be empirically recognizable. As in the case of native speakers of natural languages, they are not tied to fixed formulas, but rather can understand, speak, and discriminate between the endless varieties of necessarily innovative ways of using both old and new vocabularies to address unprecedented situations. While they may have no formal theological training, they are likely to be saturated with the language of Scripture and/or liturgy. One might, perhaps, call them flexibly devout: they have so interiorized the grammar of their religion that they are reliable judges, not directly of the doctrinal formulations (for these may be too technical for them to understand), but of the acceptability or unacceptability of the consequences of these formulations in ordinary religious life and language.

The reliability of their agreement in doctrinal matters may not improperly be called infallible. This suggestion is intended as an empirical description, not as an affirmation of faith. Think, for a moment, of what it would mean outside the Christian sphere (where we can perhaps look at the question with some detachment). A virtually unanimous and enduring agreement among flexible yet deeply pious mainstream Muslims throughout the world on some at one time disputed point of Koranic doctrine would constitute empirically indisputable evidence from a detached, non-Muslim scholarly point of view that the doctrine is not in contradiction to the inner logic of Islam. Admittedly the practical difficulties of verifying the existence of such a consensus may be insuperable. Nevertheless, as in the case of grammar, a kind of unshakable empirical certitude is theoretically available and asymptotically approachable even in reference to previously unsettled doctrinal questions. There is nothing odd about this, for we have similar certainties regarding other types of empirical knowledge, such as laws of mechanics, motion, and gravity, not to mention the sun always rising in the east, or heavy objects always falling to the surface of the earth unless they are interfered with. It is not psychologically or rhetorically strange to say that these principles, even when imperfectly formulated, are infallible and infallibly known. There is no reason for denying a similar certitude to religious doctrines. They also, given a cultural-linguistic approach, are matters of empirical knowledge. They can be infallibly known as "Christian," as "intrasystematically" even if not "ontologically" true. (The latter kind of certainty is of a logically different kind, for it is faith in the Christian message, not knowledge about it.)[17]

When considering the implications of this analysis, as we shall now do in concluding this discussion, there are two sets of questions that arise. First: Is the certitude thus attributed to doctrine theologically sufficient? Second: What about the locus of infallibility, of the authority that guarantees doctrines?

In reference to certitude, the question is whether an empirically describable variety, however strong, is religiously sufficient. Do not the believers need an assurance greater than can be provided by "natural reason" for the conviction that the church does not err in its opposition to slavery, its Christological and Trinitarian decision, its rejection of Pelagianism, and its acceptance of the possibility of infant baptism, not to mention a multitude of other matters? Do not believers depend on the infallible testimony of the Holy Spirit, or of Scripture, or of the magisterium, rather than on an empirically based confidence that the *consensus fidelium* cannot mortally err?

The objection acquires its force, I suspect, partly from a failure to understand, partly from a modern prejudice, and partly from a theological error. The failure is that of not distinguishing, as we have done, between grammatical (or intrasystematic) and ontological truth. The question is, "What is Christian?" and not, "Is Christianity true?" It is primarily the second and not the first query which requires for its answer what is now fashionably called existential commitment and what was traditionally termed supernatural faith. To be sure, those for whom Christianity is true, who are skilled in speaking and living its language, know better in practice what is Christian than does the non-Christian; but judging the Christian or non-Christian character of doctrines is an enterprise at which the unbeliever may be competent. Similarly, defective command of English is compatible with greater grammatical expertise in determining what rules native speakers follow than those speakers themselves possess.

The modern prejudice that I have in mind is Cartesian. Certitude, it is supposed, must be able to overcome universal doubt. Actually, however, as many thinkers unite in reminding us,[18] certitude always comes first. It is the precondition for doubt. To doubt what is generally accepted is unreal and unreasonable, an emotion or a pathology, unless there are statable reasons for doubting (such as, for example, a conflict in evidence or in authorities). Atheists agree with church people that the affirmations in the Apostles' Creed are authentically Christian beliefs. That agreement, unless one has specifiable reasons for raising questions in regard to particular articles, makes it foolish to doubt that these are indeed normatively Christian.[19]

The theological error that makes us question the proposition is, as could be guessed, the wrong kind of supernaturalism. Reason and nature, empirical certitude and the assurance of faith—these are not sharply divided, watertight compartments. To say that theological judgments as to the correctness of doctrinal decisions regarding the inner logic of the faith are on one level just as empirical as those which the grammarian makes when plying his or her trade is not to deny that God is active. God will not withhold his guidance from theologians who pray for it, and perhaps not even from some who do not pray, but neither does he withhold it from grammarians. For all these reasons, it is admissible for believers to say that while infallible knowledge of the authenticity of the *regulae* can on one level be analyzed as natural, it is also supernatural: a free, unmerited gift of grace.

In reference to the locus of infallibility, our model suggests, as we have said, that this locus is the whole community of competent speakers of a language. This sounds more Eastern Orthodox than either traditionally Protestant or traditionally Roman Catholic.[20] Infallibility for the Orthodox belongs to the church as a whole insofar as it is open to the Spirit and is united in space and time with all faithful witnesses from scriptural times to the present. It does not have a privileged localization in the Bible, after the Protestant manner, nor in the official magisterium, as Catholics have said. Not even ecumenical councils are infallible by themselves, but only insofar as their decrees are received by the churches. Does this mean, then, that the *sola scriptura,* on the one hand, or papal and conciliar infallibility, on the other, are simply incompatible with a rule theory of doctrine? Does the theory exclude certain theological options after all?

To draw this conclusion would be to forget the importance of situations and the possibility of conditional doctrines. The Orthodox view is appropriate when the church is undivided, whereas both Roman Catholics and Protestants have sought to define authorities, ultimate courts of appeal, that would be operationally effective when the church is divided. This has been to their advantage. They have not been frozen into traditionalistic immobility to the same degree as the East, an immobility not unrelated to the lack of a theory of final authority appropriate to a broken Christendom. Thus, in terms of our doctrinal typology, both an exclusivist *sola scriptura* and the Roman Catholic emphasis on the official magisterium could be viewed as conditionally necessary but reversible doctrines. When the church as a whole is not available as a court of last appeal—so it could be argued—it is the lesser evil to locate infallibility in Scripture or the magisterium rather than to say there is no way of deciding new issues, as the Orthodox in effect have done (they, to be sure, can always answer that Roman authoritarianism and Protestant fissiparousness are excessive prices to pay for escape from the kind of doctrinal impotence from which the East has suffered).

Moreover, these doctrines can be reinterpreted. Protestants can say that Scripture must be listened to as the final authority, but in the company of all those at all times and places who take the biblical story seriously. If one does not listen to those who have listened, one is not in fact genuinely committed to listening. Catholics can point out that the conditions under which the pope can act with "that infallibility with which Christ has endowed the church" (DS 3074) have never been fully specified, and that perhaps one of the unmentioned conditions is precisely that he seek seriously to be a spokesman for the whole church and not just for a part of it. In both cases, to the degree that the church is reunited, the operational consequences on the level of usage would coincide with what the Orthodox recommend. The three theories of infallibility, of how rightness in doctrinal matters is guaranteed, would thus become diverse formulations of the same rule, or at least compatible rules of action.

This might seem an excessively easy way of resolving conflicts over papal and scriptural infallibility, but it is not sleight of hand. If doctrines are rules, then it follows that they will often be reconcilable in circumstances where propositional truths remain adamantly opposed. This is not the kind of irenicism in which all differences are dissolved into a vague blur, into that night (as Hegel described Schelling) where all cows are black. Rules are sometimes in ineluctable collision when applied in the same situation, as the contradictions between British and American traffic regulations remind us, but not when their areas of application are distinct. It is simply that the logic of rules and of propositions is different.

Vatican I on infallibility involves such a collision, and it will continue to do so unless the churches are reunited. No matter how minimalistically interpreted, its teaching means at the very least, even on rule theory, that the dogmatic decisions of the Roman Catholic Church are not irremediably wrong. However disastrous they may seem, they will turn out for the best or, at any rate, not separate the church from the faith. Thus to accept this doctrine of infallibility is to be authorized and obligated to remain in the Roman Catholic communion no matter how much one disapproves of some of its doctrines. One is committed to understanding these doctrines in the best possible way (although this may be, on occasion, simply as the lesser of two evils), and to working, perhaps without visible success yet with hope, to overcome their defects. This may be confidence *contre coeur,* yet it is confidence. It is trust that the Protestant not only does not have but is doctrinally excluded from having in any particular church or ecclesiastical office. The Protestant can perhaps have a comparable trust in the *consensus scripturae et patrium* and in a reunited church of the future, but this is too vague to function as a usable final court of appeal in the present. For that the Protestant turns to some form of the *sola scriptura,* but this also presents grave difficulties, even though they are different from those of magisterial infallibility. Thus the Roman, Reformation, and Orthodox positions on infallibility continue to be irreconcilable in the present situation. Rule theory neither reconciles them nor legislates that one is to be preferred to the others.

This means, however, that rule theory should be doctrinally acceptable to Roman Catholics as well as to members of other communions. It seems not to contravene any of the dogmas of the major historic traditions, and it provides a framework within which ecumenical agreements and disagreements can be meaningfully discussed. This conclusion makes it possible for us to turn in the remainder of this chapter to a comparison of regulative and modern propositional views. As in the last section of the third chapter, it will here be impossible entirely to avoid technicalities.

IV
THE SUPERIORITY OF A REGULATIVE VIEW

The agreements between regulative and contemporary propositional views of the nature of doctrine are in some respects more striking than the disagreements. Both Lonergan and Rahner,[21] to use them as examples, do not deny that doctrines are rules. Practical doctrines cannot be anything else; and given Lonergan's references in recent writings to the "affective" character of doctrines of the Marian type,[22] he at least might be open to the suggestion in section II of this chapter that these be treated as instantiations of rules rather than as having a statable, fixed propositional content. Even in the area of the early creeds there is considerable convergence. Here Rahner and Lonergan give a first-order ontological or metaphysical propositional interpretation, but Lonergan also adds, it will be recalled, a regulative account of the emergence of Trinitarian and Christological doctrines.

In this last instance, the contemporary propositionalism represented by someone like Lonergan is intermediate between the classical variety and a consistently regulative theory of doctrine. For most medieval and post-medieval theologians, a doctrine is a rule only because it is first of all a proposition. It is, for example, because Father and Son are ontologically consubstantial that the Christian discourse must conform to the Athanasian rule (to which we have already referred) that whatever is said of the Father must be said of the Son, except that the Son is not the Father. Lonergan's historical work reverses this relation. The regulative function was first to be clearly perceived, and only subsequently with the rise of scholasticism was the metaphysical import fully grasped and affirmed. He therefore agrees with rule theory that the doctrinal authority, not only of practical norms but also of creedal affirmations, does not necessarily depend on first-order ontological reference.

There are other points of agreement. We earlier cited both Luther and Newman to the effect that what is essential to the church in one situation may not be in another. This awareness is intense among most contemporary theologians. It follows that what is doctrinally significant varies from age to age. What is vital in one context may become peripheral in another, and vice versa. New doctrines may develop and old ones be forgotten (although the logic of taking doctrines as propositional truths suggests that this last point should be regretted rather than accepted). Second, Lonergan and other propositionalists now generally insist in opposition to classical positions that, although a doctrinal proposition is permanent, its formulation may vary greatly from period to period and from culture to culture. Because of these considerations, modified or historicized propositional theories seem no less capable of admitting historical change and diversity than is a rule theory (although, as we shall note, they do so in peculiarly complicated ways).

Thus, as is often true in theoretical disputes, the practical consequences of the disagreement are in some respects minor. Except in the case of extremely high velocities or extremely large or small masses, Newtonian and Einsteinian physics produce much the same results. Similarly, if the comparison may be allowed, when propositional and regulative theories try to account for much the same doctrinal data in the context of modern views of history and culture, their differences on concrete issues are likely to be marginal. Yet there are differences, and for some purposes these are important.

The major theoretical dispute, to start with that, turns on the proper application of Ockham's razor. From the regulative perspective, propositional interpretations are superfluous. If doctrines such as that of Nicaea can be enduringly normative as rules, there is no reason to proceed further and insist on an ontological reference.

The issue is a narrow one. Rule theory does not prohibit speculations on the possible correspondence of the Trinitarian pattern of Christian language to the metaphysical structure of the Godhead, but simply says that these are not doctrinally necessary and cannot be binding. They are like discussions of whether there is a substance-attribute structure of finite entities corresponding to the subject-predicate structure of sentences. Some philosophers, such as Aristotle, hold that there is (and I, for one, am enough of an Aristotelian to be inclined to agree), but this is irrelevant to the linguist. Whether Aristotle is right or wrong makes no difference for most purposes to the subject-predicate way in which we must speak in order to make sense of the world; and similarly, ontological interpretations of the Trinity do not, or should not, be made communally normative for the way Christians live and think.

A comparison with scientific theories may also be helpful. These, like Trinitarian and Christological theories, need not be given a metaphysical interpretation, although in both cases it might be legitimate for certain purposes to give such an interpretation. Aristotelian, Newtonian, and Einsteinian theories of space and time, for example, are evaluated scientifically quite independently of the metaphysical question of which is closer to the way things really are. If relativity is ontologically true, then both Aristotle and Einstein are on this point superior to Newton with his notion of space and time as absolutes. Scientifically—e.g., for predictive purposes—Newton's position, however, is superior to Aristotle's and inferior to Einstein's. Similarly, theological theories that tend to identify the economic and immanent trinities, as do those of Rahner and much of the Eastern tradition,[23] may or may not correspond better to the triune reality of God than do the Augustinian and Thomistic theories that Lonergan prefers, which stress the immanent trinity of psychological analogies and substantial relations.[24] That question is unanswerable this side of the Eschaton. It is also irrelevant to theological assessment. Which theory is theologically best depends on how well it organizes the data of Scripture and tradition with a view to their use in Christian worship and life. In terms of these specifically theological criteria, there may be good or bad theories on both sides of the ontological dispute regarding the economic and immanent aspects of the Trinity. The question of the ontological reference of the theories may often be unimportant for theological evaluation.

The application of these considerations to Trinitarian doctrine is evident. If the doctrine is a rule or conjunction of rules for, among other things, the construction of Trinitarian theories, then both types of theory we have mentioned can be doctrinally correct, providing they conform to the same rules. If, however, the doctrine is a proposition with ontological reference, only one type of theory has a chance of being true because the theories disagree on what the ontological reference is.

This is not simply a technical divergence: the practical disadvantages of the propositional view are considerable. The propositional view suggests that one of the two main streams of Christian theological thinking about the Trinity is unwittingly heretical, even though the church has not yet made up its mind which one. Given this grave implication, there must be very good reasons indeed for saying that the doctrine of the Trinity is propositional as well as regulative, but it is not at all apparent that either party to the dispute has even attempted to supply them.

Perhaps the best way to sum up the practical difference between propositional and regulative approaches is by considering the contrast between interpreting a truth and obeying a rule.[25] If, to shift examples, the immortality of the soul is a first-order proposition, then those who stand in a tradition for which this has been doctrine, but find its mind-body dualism unacceptable, are obligated to discover what truth it enunciates, however improbable this truth may seem from the dualistic viewpoint of the original formulators.[26] They are virtually forced into that endless process of speculative reinterpretation which is the main stock-in-trade of much contemporary theology, both Protestant and Catholic. If the doctrine, in contrast, is taken as a rule, attention is focused on the concrete life and language of the community. Because the doctrine is to be followed rather than interpreted, the theologian's task is to specify the circumstances, whether temporary or enduring, in which it applies. In the first case, as Wittgenstein might say, language idles without doing any work, while in the second case, the gears mesh with reality and theological reflection on doctrine becomes directly relevant to the praxis of the church. The question raised in reference to Nicaea and Chalcedon is not how they can be interpreted in modern categories, but rather how contemporary Christians can do as well or better in maximizing the Jesus Christ of the biblical narratives as the way to the one God of whom the Bible speaks. Such considerations suggest that rule theory, instead of undermining the authority of doctrines, may be better adapted to enhancing their regulative efficacy than are modernized and relativizing propositional interpretations.

Thus the outcome of this discussion is a higher estimate of a rule theory of doctrine than our argument strictly requires. We started by asking whether a regulative view could be as satisfactory as a propositional one in allowing for the possibility of doctrinal normativeness and permanence, but the conclusion is that it is superior on at least the first point. The focus on praxis, and the opposition to the doctrinal relevance (though not necessarily

to the intellectual enjoyment) of metaphysically oriented theological speculation, makes it easier to specify what is normative about doctrines. The
time has now come, therefore, to discuss in more detail the consequences
for theological work of the theory of religion and doctrine that we have been
exploring.

NOTES

1. For the most recent widely discussed attack on the doctrine of the ancient
creeds, see John Hick (ed.), *The Myth of God Incarnate* (Westminster Press, 1977).
For a critical review, see George Lindbeck, *Journal of Religion* 60/2 (1980), pp.
149–151.

2. Like many other contemporary authors, Don Cupitt disregards this polyva-
lence of symbols and stresses only the negative psychosocial import of the doctrine
of the incarnation. (See Hick [ed.], *The Myth of God Incarnate,* pp. 133–147.)

3. This insight is reflected indirectly in the term *regula fidei* and becomes explicit
in the Athanasian dictum cited below. For the development from the New Testament via the rule of faith to the old Roman symbol and later creeds see J. N. D.
Kelly, *Early Christian Creeds,* 3d ed. (London: Longmans, Green, 1972).

4. Bernard Lonergan, *De Deo Trino* (Rome: Gregorian University Press, 1964).
Part of this work has been published in English translation: *The Way to Nicea,* tr.
by Conn O'Donovan (Westminster Press, 1976). See also "The Dehellenization of
Dogma," in Lonergan's *A Second Collection* (London: Darton, Longman & Todd,
1974; Philadelphia: Westminster Press, 1975); and see his *Method in Theology*
(Herder & Herder, 1972), pp. 307ff.

5. Lonergan, *Method in Theology,* p. 307.

6. Ibid., p. 308.

7. Ibid., p. 309. Cf. for this paragraph the fuller discussion in "Dehellenization,"
ibid., pp. 23ff.

8. In what follows I use "principle" and "rule" interchangeably because the three
doctrinal rules of which we are here speaking function much as does, e.g., the
principle of causality. The latter as normally employed makes a truth claim ("everything has a cause"), but one that functions as a warrant and directive for inquiry
rather than being in any sense a proposition that can be tested. Cf. John H. Whit-
taker, *Matters of Faith and Matters of Principle: Religious Truth Claims and Their
Logic* (Trinity University Press, 1981).

9. Arianism is hard to assess because evidence is accumulating that the reason
some Arians denied the *homoousion* may have been, not that they had a more
Hellenistic view of the divine transcendence and oneness than their opponents, but
that they were more insistent on the fullness with which the divine Son participates
in the human condition. (See Marcel Richard [ed. and tr.], *Thirty-One Homilies of
Asterius* [1956]. For this reference I am indebted to an unpublished paper of Maurice

Wiles titled "Early Arianism Revisited.") If so, it could be argued against the traditional interpretation that the Arian concern was a biblical soteriological one rather than a metaphysical concern extraneous to the scriptural message. This suggests the hypothesis that both the Arians and their opponents shared a biblically unacceptable view of the divine transcendence and impassibility which made it impossible to maintain both the *homoousion* and what Luther was later to call a *theologia crucis.* Only when the unbiblical assumptions regarding the divine oneness and transcendence are surrendered can the Athanasian and the (putative) Arian concerns be combined. It is as yet too early to tell whether some such revision of the traditional interpretation of Arianism will prove necessary. J. Pelikan, in *The Christian Tradition,* Vol. 1 (University of Chicago Press, 1971), for example, continues to present the older view.

10. The argument is not that Christians of the first centuries consciously reasoned in terms of the three principles any more than speakers of natural languages consciously follow grammatical rules. In both cases, however, the adequacy of attempts to formulate the rules can be tested by whether they in fact describe or "predict" the usages, especially the innovative ones, that prove acceptable or unacceptable in a given community. The principles I have suggested, therefore, have the status of testable historical hypotheses. One needs to ask, for example, whether in the context of the times there was any plausible way of asserting that Jesus Christ is one being who is both true God and true man other than something like the "one person in two natures" of Chalcedon. It may well be, as Maurice Wiles has argued (*Working Papers in Doctrine* [London: SCM Press, 1976], pp. 38–49, esp. p. 47) that this formulation was necessary because of the strong Greek emphasis on God's total impassibility. As this emphasis, however, was presupposed by everyone rather than being itself a subject of discussion or decision, it can from the present perspective (in contrast to the one Wiles adopts) be regarded as a conditioning factor in the application of the rules, rather than as a fourth principle which was itself affirmed. More detailed historical studies of such issues are, to be sure, necessary. In their absence, I simply record my impression that the available historical data can be plausibly construed in terms of the three principles I have enumerated. In any case, even if doubts are raised about the number and character of the principles as I have described them, it seems clear that the notion of something like grammatical principles or pressures is needed in order to conceptualize the continuities amid discontinuities that characterized early Christian thought. Words such as "objective" and "aim," which authors such as Wiles use to speak of the continuities (Maurice Wiles, *The Making of Christian Doctrine* [Cambridge: Cambridge University Press, 1967], pp. 172–173), have the disadvantage of being drawn from the language of conscious intentionality, with the result that the abiding factor consists simply of "the continuation of the same task of interpreting the Church's Scriptures, her worship and her experience of salvation" (ibid., p. 181). Such a formulation can be given an acceptable construal, but as it stands, it is too vague to suggest any historically testable hypotheses, and when combined with such terms as "aim" and "objective," it has the defect of suggesting some kind of collective purpose. A more impersonal terminology is needed. In the context of mundane history, even if not of theology,

it would be a mistake to speak as if there were a communal will that moved Christian thinking in a particular doctrinal direction over a long period of time. It makes more empirical sense to ask if this direction can be accounted for by certain logical features of the religious language instantiated in Scripture and worship. What guided development, one might say, was the avoidance of cognitive dissonance rather than positive collective desires.

11. Lonergan, *Method in Theology,* p. 320.

12. Karl Rahner, "The Immaculate Conception," in his *Theological Investigations,* Vol. 1 (London: Darton, Longman & Todd, 1961), pp. 201–214; "Interpretation of the Doctrine of the Assumption," ibid., pp. 215–228. The freedom with which Rahner speculates in these essays on the possible doctrinal significance of the Marian dogmas is the inspiration rather than the source of the following paragraphs.

13. For the questioning of the Western (Augustinian) teaching on sin, see Piet Schoonenberg, *Man and Sin: A Theological View* (University of Notre Dame Press, 1972); George Vandervelde, *Original Sin: Two Major Trends in Contemporary Roman Catholic Reinterpretation* (Amsterdam: Rodopi, 1975).

14. For discussions of infallibility containing references to the literature, see George Lindbeck, *Infallibility* (Marquette University Press, 1972); in J. J. Kirvan (ed.), *The Infallibility Debate* (Paulist Press, 1971), pp. 107–152; "The Reformation and the Infallibility Debate," in P. and C. Empie and A. Murphy (eds.), *Teaching Authority and Infallibility in the Church* (Augsburg Publishing House, 1980), pp. 101–119. The entirety of the last-named volume is relevant. For a Roman Catholic study of the problem that reaches conclusions often parallel to mine, but by a more "Lonerganian" route, see Peter Chirico, *Infallibility: The Crossroads of Doctrine* (Sheed, Andrews & McMeel, 1977).

15. Karl Rahner, *Theological Investigations,* Vol. 6 (Helicon Press, 1970), p. 308.

16. Protestants sometimes defend the double predestinarianism of the Reformers on these grounds, and Catholics, the definition of papal infallibility at Vatican I.

17. See Chapter 3, section IV, above, for the distinction between intrasystematic and ontological truth.

18. For a nice characterization of the defects of the method of universal doubt, see Bernard Lonergan, *Insight* (Harper & Row, 1978), pp. 408–411. Cf. his *Method in Theology,* pp. 41–47.

19. This comment is not meant to challenge the legitimacy of, for example, arguing that "Virgin," in "born of the Virgin Mary," functions as an identifying appellation rather than as an affirmation. In any case, the argument at this point is that those who have reservations about the place of a doctrine in the authoritative corpus of Christian beliefs should do so for specific reasons (e.g., in reference to the virgin birth, the literary character of the Gospel infancy narratives) rather than because of a generalized critical attitude.

20. For an Eastern Orthodox treatment of infallibility, see Nicolas Afanassieff in O. Rousseau and J. J. von Allmen (eds.), *L'Infaillibilité de l'Eglise* (Gembloux: Chevetogne, 1963), pp. 183–201.

21. See the comments on "mixed" or "two-dimensional" approaches in Chapter 1, section I, above.

22. Lonergan, *Method in Theology,* p. 320.

23. Karl Rahner, *The Trinity,* tr. by Joseph Donceel (Herder & Herder, 1970). For Rahner's view of the relation of his position to that of the Greeks, see pp. 16–18, esp. n. 13; and for his criticism of psychological theories, including a reference to Lonergan, see pp. 96–97.

24. Bernard Lonergan, *De Deo Trino* (Rome: Gregorian University Press, 1964).

25. Ludwig Wittgenstein notes that "there is a way of grasping a rule which is not an interpretation, but which is exhibited in what we call 'obeying the rule' and 'going against it' in actual cases" (*Philosophical Investigations* [Macmillan Co., 1973], #201). Cf. further: "Any interpretation still hangs in the air along with what it interprets, and cannot give any support. Interpretations by themselves do not determine meaning" (#198).

26. See Chapter 4, n. 23, above, for a typical, though random, example.

CHAPTER 6

TOWARD A POSTLIBERAL THEOLOGY

This final chapter is an addendum to the main argument of the book, but a necessary one. If the theory of religion we have been exploring is useful only for understanding church doctrine and not also in other theological areas, it will ultimately prove unacceptable even to specialists in doctrine. In this chapter, therefore, we shall discuss the implications for theological method of a cultural-linguistic approach to religion, starting with some preliminary observations on the meaning and difficulties of assessing, as we shall afterward do, the faithfulness, applicability, and intelligibility of fundamentally different types of theology.

I
THE PROBLEM OF ASSESSMENT

Systematic or dogmatic theology has generally been thought of in the Christian West as especially concerned with faithfulness, practical theology with applicability, and foundational or apologetic theology with intelligibility; but each of these concerns is present in every theological discipline. When dogmaticians attempt faithfully to describe the normative features of a religion, they are also interested in applicability and intelligibility. Similarly, practical and foundational theologians seek not only to apply and make the religion intelligible but also to be faithful.

Further specification of the meaning of these terms depends on the contexts in which they are employed. Theologies of a given type, whether this be preliberal propositionalist, liberal experiential-expressivist, or postliberal cultural-linguistic, can combine formal similarities with radical material differences in their understanding of faithfulness, applicability, and intelligibility. Spanish inquisitors and Enlightenment theologians disagreed radi-

cally in creed and practice and yet agreed on the formal point that propositional truth is the decisive test of adequacy. Similarly, Anglo-Catholics such
as the authors of *Lux Mundi,* Lutheran confessionalists of the Erlangen
school, and some "death of God" theologians shared the liberal commitment to the primacy of experience but differed on the material question of
what kind of experiences are religiously crucial. Analogously, a Christian
postliberal consensus on the primarily cultural-linguistic character of religions would not by itself overcome substantive disagreements between conservatives and progressives, feminists and antifeminists, Catholics and Protestants. The debates would turn more on conceptual or grammatical
considerations than on experiential or propositional ones, but they would
also involve disagreements on where proper grammar is to be found, on who
are the competent speakers of a religious language. The progressives would
appeal to rebels, the conservatives to establishments, and Catholics and
Protestants would continue to differ in their understanding of the relation
of Scripture and tradition. Nevertheless, the common framework would
make possible, though not guarantee, genuine arguments over the relative
adequacy of specifiably different positions.

Such arguments are difficult, however, when theologies have formally
different views of religion. The problem, as we have noted in earlier chapters, is that each type of theology is embedded in a conceptual framework
so comprehensive that it shapes its own criteria of adequacy. Thus what
propositionalists with their stress on unchanging truth and falsity regard as
faithful, applicable, and intelligible is likely to be dismissed as dead orthodoxy by liberal experiential-expressivists. Conversely, the liberal claim
that change and pluralism in religious expression are necessary for intelligibility, applicability, and faithfulness is attacked by the propositionally orthodox as an irrationally relativistic and practically self-defeating betrayal
of the faith. A postliberal might propose to overcome this polarization
between tradition and innovation by a distinction between abiding doctrinal
grammar and variable theological vocabulary, but this proposal appears
from other perspectives as the worst of two worlds rather than the best of
both. In view of this situation, the most that can be done in this chapter
is to comment on how faithfulness, applicability, and intelligibility might
be understood in postliberal theologies,[1] and then leave it to the readers to
make their own assessments.

II
FAITHFULNESS AS INTRATEXTUALITY

The task of descriptive (dogmatic or systematic) theology is to give a
normative explication of the meaning a religion has for its adherents. One

way of pursuing this task that is compatible with a cultural-linguistic approach is what I shall call "intratextual," while an "extratextual" method is natural for those whose understanding of religion is propositional or experiential-expressive. The latter locates religious meaning outside the text or semiotic system either in the objective realities to which it refers or in the experiences it symbolizes, whereas for cultural-linguists the meaning is immanent. Meaning is constituted by the uses of a specific language rather than being distinguishable from it. Thus the proper way to determine what "God" signifies, for example, is by examining how the word operates within a religion and thereby shapes reality and experience rather than by first establishing its propositional or experiential meaning and reinterpreting or reformulating its uses accordingly. It is in this sense that theological description in the cultural-linguistic mode is intrasemiotic or intratextual.

In an extended or improper sense, something like intratextuality is characteristic of the descriptions of not only religion but also other forms of rule-governed human behavior from carpentry and mathematics to languages and cultures. Hammers and saws, ordinals and numerals, winks and signs of the cross, words and sentences are made comprehensible by indicating how they fit into systems of communication or purposeful action, not by reference to outside factors. One does not succeed in identifying the 8:02 to New York by describing the history or manufacture of trains or even by a complete inventory of the cars, passengers, and conductors that constituted and traveled on it on a given day. None of the cars, passengers, and crew might be the same the next day, and yet the train would be self-identically the 8:02 to New York. Its meaning, its very reality, is its function within a particular transportation system. Much the same can be said of winks and signs of the cross: they are quite distinct from nonmeaningful but physically identical eye twitches and hand motions, and their reality as meaningful signs is wholly constituted in any individual occurrence by their intratextuality, by their place, so to speak, in a story.

Meaning is more fully intratextual in semiotic systems (composed, as they entirely are, of interpretive and communicative signs, symbols, and actions) than in other forms of ruled human behavior such as carpentry or transportation systems; but among semiotic systems, intratextuality (though still in an extended sense) is greatest in natural languages, cultures, and religions which (unlike mathematics, for example) are potentially all-embracing and possess the property of reflexivity. One can speak of all life and reality in French, or from an American or a Jewish perspective; and one can also describe French in French, American culture in American terms, and Judaism in Jewish ones. This makes it possible for theology to be intratextual, not simply by explicating religion from within but in the stronger sense of describing everything as inside, as interpreted by the religion, and doing this by means of religiously shaped second-order concepts.

In view of their comprehensiveness, reflexivity, and complexity, religions require what Clifford Geertz, borrowing a term from Gilbert Ryle, has called "thick description,"[2] and which he applies to culture, but with the understanding that it also holds for religion. A religion cannot be treated as a formalizable "symbolic system . . . by isolating its elements, specifying the internal relationships among these elements, and then characterizing the whole system in some general way—according to the core symbols around which it is organized, the underlying structures of which it is the surface expression, or the ideological principles upon which it is based. . . . This hermetic approach to things seems to me to run the danger of locking . . . analysis away from its proper object, the informal logic of actual life." The theologian, like the ethnographer, should approach "such broader interpretations and abstract analyses from the direction of exceedingly extended acquaintances with extremely small matters." "As interlocked systems of construable signs . . . culture [including religion] is not a power, something to which social events, behaviors, institutions, or processes can be causally attributed; it is a context, something within which they can be intelligibly—that is, thickly—described." Only by detailed "familiarity with the imaginative universe in which . . . acts are signs" can one diagnose or specify the meaning of these acts for the adherents of a religion. What the theologian needs to explicate "is a multiplicity of complex conceptual structures, many of them superimposed or knotted into one another, which are at once strange, irregular and inexplicit, and which he must contrive somehow first to grasp and then to render." In rendering the salient features, the essential task "is not to codify abstract regularities but to make thick description possible, not to generalize across cases but to generalize within them." If this is not done, one may think, for example, that Roman and Confucian *gravitas* are much the same, or that atheistic Marxism more nearly resembles atheistic Buddhism than biblical theism. This is as egregious an error as supposing that uninflected English is closer to uninflected Chinese than to German.

Thick description, it should be noted, is not to be confused with Baconian empiricism, with sticking to current facts. It is rather the full range of the interpretive medium which needs to be exhibited, and because this range in the case of religion is potentially all-encompassing, description has a creative aspect. There is, indeed, no more demanding exercise of the inventive and imaginative powers than to explore how a language, culture, or religion may be employed to give meaning to new domains of thought, reality, and action. Theological description can be a highly constructive enterprise.

Finally, in the instance of religions more than any other type of semiotic system, description is not simply metaphorically but literally intratextual. This is true in some degree of all the world's major faiths. They all have relatively fixed canons of writings that they treat as exemplary or normative instantiations of their semiotic codes. One test of faithfulness for all of them is the degree to which descriptions correspond to the semiotic universe paradigmatically encoded in holy writ.

The importance of texts and of intratextuality for theological faithfulness becomes clearer when we consider the unwritten religions of nonliterate societies. Evans-Pritchard[3] tells of a Nuer tribesman who excitedly reported to him that a woman in the village had given birth to twins, both dead, and that one was a hippopotamus and had been placed in a stream, and the other a bird and had been placed in a tree. There are in that society no canonical documents to consult in order to locate these puzzling events within the wider contexts that give them meaning. Is the equation of dead twins with birds and hippopotami central or peripheral to Nuer thought and life? Would the religion and culture be gravely disturbed if this equation were eliminated? Even the wisest of Evans-Pritchard's informants might not have understood these questions, and even if they did, they presumably would have had no idea of how to reach a consensus in answering them. In oral cultures there is no transpersonal authority to which the experts on tradition can refer their disputes. This helps explain why purely customary religions and cultures readily dissolve under the pressure of historical, social, and linguistic change, but it also suggests that canonical texts are a condition, not only for the survival of a religion but for the very possibility of normative theological description. In any case, whether or not this is universally true, the intrasemiotic character of descriptive theology is inseparable from intratextuality in the three Western monotheisms—Judaism, Christianity, and Islam. These are preeminently religions of the book.

We need now to speak in more detail of how to interpret a text in terms of its immanent meanings—that is, in terms of the meanings immanent in the religious language of whose use the text is a paradigmatic instance. On the informal level this is not a problem; it becomes so, as we shall see, only when theology becomes alienated from those ways of reading classics,[4] whether religious or nonreligious, which seem natural within a given culture or society. Masterpieces such as *Oedipus Rex* and *War and Peace,* for example, evoke their own domains of meaning. They do so by what they themselves say about the events and personages of which they tell. In order to understand them in their own terms, there is no need for extraneous references to, for example, Freud's theories or historical treatments of the Napoleonic wars. Further, such works shape the imagination and perceptions of the attentive reader so that he or she forever views the world to some extent through the lenses they supply. To describe the basic meaning of these books is an intratextual task, a matter of explicating their contents and the perspectives on extratextual reality that they generate.[5]

These same considerations apply even more forcefully to the preeminently authoritative texts that are the canonical writings of religious communities. For those who are steeped in them, no world is more real than the ones they create. A scriptural world is thus able to absorb the universe. It supplies the interpretive framework within which believers seek to live their lives and understand reality. This happens quite apart from formal theories. Augustine did not describe his work in the categories we are employing, but the whole of his theological production can be understood as a progressive, even if not always successful, struggle to insert everything from Platonism and the Pelagian problem to the fall of Rome into the world of the Bible. Aquinas tried to do something similar with Aristotelianism, and Schleiermacher with German romantic idealism. The way they described extrascriptural realities and experience, so it can be argued, was shaped by biblical categories much more than was warranted by their formal methodologies.

In the case of Aquinas especially, however, the shaping was in part methodologically legitimated. Traditional exegetical procedures (of which he gives one of the classic descriptions[6]) assume that Scripture creates its own domain of meaning and that the task of interpretation is to extend this over the whole of reality. The particular ways of doing this depend, to be sure, on the character of the religion and its texts. One set of interpretive techniques is appropriate when the Torah is the center of the scripture, another when it is the story of Jesus, and still another when it is the Buddha's enlightenment and teachings. For the most part, we shall limit our observations on this point to the Christian case.

Here there was a special though not exclusive emphasis on typological or figural devices, first to unify the canon, and second to encompass the cosmos. Typology was used to incorporate the Hebrew Scriptures into a canon that focused on Christ, and then, by extension, to embrace extrabiblical reality. King David, for example, was in some respects a typological foreshadowing of Jesus, but he was also, in Carolingian times, a type for Charlemagne and, in Reformation days, as even Protestants said, for Charles V in his wars against the Turks. Thus an Old Testament type, filtered through the New Testament antitype, became a model for later kings and, in the case of Charlemagne, provided a documentable stimulus to the organization of the educational and parish systems that stand at the institutional origins of Western civilization. Unlike allegorizing, typological interpretation did not empty Old Testament or postbiblical personages and events of their own reality,[7] and therefore they constituted a powerful means for imaginatively incorporating all being into a Christ-centered world.

It is important to note the direction of interpretation. Typology does not make scriptural contents into metaphors for extrascriptural realities, but the other way around. It does not suggest, as is often said in our day, that believers find their stories in the Bible, but rather that they make the story of the Bible their story. The cross is not to be viewed as a figurative representation of suffering nor the messianic kingdom as a symbol for hope in the future; rather, suffering should be cruciform, and hopes for the future messianic. More generally stated, it is the religion instantiated in Scripture which defines being, truth, goodness, and beauty, and the nonscriptural exemplifications of these realities need to be transformed into figures (or types or antitypes) of the scriptural ones. Intratextual theology redescribes reality within the scriptural framework rather than translating Scripture into extrascriptural categories. It is the text, so to speak, which absorbs the world, rather than the world the text.

There is always the danger, however, that the extrabiblical materials inserted into the biblical universe will themselves become the basic framework of interpretation. This is what happened, so the Christian mainstream concluded, in the case of Gnosticism. Here Hellenism became the interpreter rather than the interpreted. The Jewish rabbi who is the crucified and resurrected Messiah of the New Testament accounts was transformed into a mythological figure illustrative of thoroughly nonscriptural meanings. Nor did the mainstream wholly escape the danger. It creedally insisted that the Jesus spoken of in Scripture is the Lord, but it often read Scripture in so Hellenistic a way that this Jesus came to resemble a semipagan demigod. The doctrinal consensus on the primacy of Scripture, on the canonical status of the Old as well as the New Testament, and on the full humanity of Christ was not by itself enough to maintain an integrally scriptural framework within which to interpret the classical heritage which the church sought to Christianize. Better theological and exegetical procedures were needed.

Up through the Reformation, this need was in part filled through the typological methods we have already noted. As one moves in the West from Augustine, through Aquinas, to Luther and Calvin, there is an increasing resistance to indiscriminate allegorizing and an insistence on the primacy of a specifiable literal intratextual sense. Whatever the failures in actual execution, and they were many, the interpretive direction was from the Bible to the world rather than vice versa.

In the Reformers, it should be noted, the resistance to allegorizing and the greater emphasis on intratextuality *(scriptura sui ipsius interpres)* did not diminish but heightened the emphasis on proclamation, on the preached word. Scripture, one might say, was interpreted by its use,[8] by the *viva vox evangelii.* In the intratextual context, this emphasis on the living word involves applying the language, concepts, and categories of Scripture to contemporary realities, and is different in its intellectual, practical, and homiletical consequences from liberal attempts, of which Ebeling's is the most notable,[9] to understand the Reformation notion of the word of God in terms of an experiential "word event."

As the work of Hans Frei shows,[10] the situation has changed radically in recent centuries, and new difficulties have arisen. Typological interpretation collapsed under the combined onslaughts of rationalistic, pietistic, and historical-critical developments. Scripture ceased to function as the lens through which theologians viewed the world and instead became primarily an object of study whose religiously significant or literal meaning was located outside itself. The primarily literary approaches of the past with their affinities to informal ways of reading the classics in their own terms were replaced by fundamentalist, historical-critical, and expressivist preoccupations with facticity or experience. The intratextual meanings of Scripture continue informally to shape the imagination of the West (even atheistic Marxists think of history as the unfolding of a determinate pattern with an ultimately ineluctable outcome), but theologians do not make these meanings methodologically primary. Instead, if they are existentially inclined, they reinterpret the notion of providential guidance, for example, as a symbolic expression of confidence in the face of the vicissitudes of life; or, if they objectivize, they might, as did Teilhard de Chardin, interpret providence in terms of an optimistic version of evolutionary science. Whether it will be possible to regain a specifically biblical understanding of providence depends in part on the possibility of theologically reading Scripture once again in literary rather than nonliterary ways.

The depth of the present crisis is best seen when one considers that even those who doctrinally agree that the story of Jesus is the key to the understanding of reality are often in fundamental theological disagreement over what the story is really about, over its normative or literal sense.[11] Is the literal meaning of the story the history it is on some readings supposed to record, and if so, is this history that of the fundamentalist or of the historical critic? Or is the real meaning, the theologically important meaning, the way of being in the world which the story symbolizes, or the liberating actions and attitudes it expresses, or the ethical ideals it instantiates, or the metaphysical truths about God-manhood it illustrates, or the gospel promises it embodies? Each of these ways of construing the story depends on a distinct interpretive framework (historical, phenomenological, existential, ethical, metaphysical, doctrinal) that specifies the questions asked of the text and shapes the pictures of Jesus that emerge. These pictures may all be formally orthodox in the sense that they are reconcilable with Nicaea, but their

implications for religious practice and understanding are radically divergent. Nothing better illustrates the point made in earlier chapters that for
most purposes theological issues are more crucial and interesting than
doctrinal ones.

The intratextual way of dealing with this problem depends heavily on
literary considerations. The normative or literal meaning must be consistent
with the kind of text it is taken to be by the community for which it is
important. The meaning must not be esoteric: not something behind, be-
neath, or in front of the text; not something that the text reveals, discloses,
implies, or suggests to those with extraneous metaphysical, historical, or
experiential interests. It must rather be what the text says in terms of the
communal language of which the text is an instantiation. A legal document
should not be treated in quasi-kabbalistic fashion as first of all a piece of
expressive symbolism (though it may secondarily be that also); nor should
the Genesis account of creation be turned fundamentalistically into science;
nor should one turn a realistic narrative (which a novel also can be) into
history (or, alternatively, as the historical critic is wont to do, into a source
of clues for the reconstruction of history). If the literary character of the
story of Jesus, for example, is that of utilizing, as realistic narratives do, the
interaction of purpose and circumstance to render the identity description
of an agent, then it is Jesus' identity as thus rendered, not his historicity,
existential significance, or metaphysical status, which is the literal and
theologically controlling meaning of the tale.[12] The implications of the story
for determining the metaphysical status, or existential significance, or historical career of Jesus Christ may have varying degrees of theological
importance, but they are not determinative. The believer, so an intratextual
approach would maintain, is not told primarily to be conformed to a recon-
structed Jesus of history (as Hans Küng maintains),[13] nor to a metaphysical
Christ of faith (as in much of the propositionalist tradition),[14] nor to an abba
experience of God (as for Schillebeeckx),[15] nor to an agapeic way of being
in the world (as for David Tracy),[16] but he or she is rather to be conformed
to the Jesus Christ depicted in the narrative. An intratextual reading tries
to derive the interpretive framework that designates the theologically controlling sense from the literary structure of the text itself.[17]

This type of literary approach can be extended to cover, not simply the
story of Jesus, but all of Scripture. What is the literary genre of the Bible
as a whole in its canonical unity? What holds together the diverse materials
it contains: poetic, prophetic, legal, liturgical, sapiential, mythical, legend-
ary, and historical? These are all embraced, it would seem, in an overarching story that has the specific literary features of realistic narrative as
exemplified in diverse ways, for example, by certain kinds of parables,
novels, and historical accounts. It is as if the Bible were a "vast, loosely-

structured, non-fictional novel" (to use a phrase David Kelsey applies to Karl Barth's view of Scripture).[18]

Further, it is possible to specify the primary function of the canonical narrative (which is also the function of many of its most important component stories from the Pentateuch to the Gospels). It is "to render a character . . . , offer an identity description of an agent,"[19] namely God. It does this, not by telling what God is in and of himself, but by accounts of the interaction of his deeds and purposes with those of creatures in their ever-changing circumstances. These accounts reach their climax in what the Gospels say of the risen, ascended, and ever-present Jesus Christ whose identity as the divine-human agent is unsubstitutably enacted in the stories of Jesus of Nazareth. The climax, however, is logically inseparable from what preceeds it. The Jesus of the Gospels is the Son of the God of Abraham, Isaac, and Jacob in the same strong sense that the Hamlet of Shakespeare's play is Prince of Denmark. In both cases, the title with its reference to the wider context irreplaceably rather than contingently identifies the bearer of the name.

It is easy to see how theological descriptions of a religion may on this view need to be materially diverse even when the formal criterion of faithfulness remains the same. The primary focus is not on God's being in itself, for that is not what the text is about, but on how life is to be lived and reality construed in the light of God's character as an agent as this is depicted in the stories of Israel and of Jesus. Life, however, is not the same in catacombs and space shuttles, and reality is different for, let us say, Platonists and Whiteheadians. Catacomb dwellers and astronauts might rightly emphasize diverse aspects of the biblical accounts of God's character and action in describing their respective situations. Judging by catacomb paintings, the first group often saw themselves as sheep in need of a shepherd, while the second group would perhaps be well advised to stress God's grant to human beings of stewardship over planet Earth. Similarly, Platonic and Whiteheadian differences over the nature of reality lead to sharp disagreements about the proper characterization of God's metaphysical properties, while antimetaphysicians, in turn, argue that no theory of divine attributes is consistent with the character of the biblical God.

Yet all these theologies could agree that God is appropriately depicted in stories about a being who created the cosmos without any humanly fathomable reason, but—simply for his own good pleasure and the pleasure of his goodness—appointed Homo sapiens stewards of one minuscule part of this cosmos, permitted appalling evils, chose Israel and the church as witnessing peoples, and sent Jesus as Messiah and Immanuel, God with us. The intention of these theologies, whether successful or unsuccessful, could in every case be to describe life and reality in ways conformable to what these stories indicate about God. They could, to repeat, have a common intratextual norm of faithfulness despite their material disagreements.

Intratextual theologies can also, however, disagree on the norm. They can dispute over whether realistic narrative is the best or only way to identify the distinctive genre and interpretive framework of the Christian canon, and, even if it is, on how to characterize the divine agent at work in the biblical stories. More fundamentally, they could disagree on the extent and unity of the canon. If Revelation and Daniel are the center of Scripture, as they seem to be for Scofield Bible premillenialists, a very different picture of God's agency and purposes emerges. Further, as current debates over feminism vividly remind us, past tradition or present consensus can serve as extensions of the canon and deeply influence the interpretation of the whole. These extensions can on occasion go beyond the specifically Christian or religious realm. The philosophical tradition from Plato to Heidegger operates as the canonical corpus for much Western reflection on God or the human condition; and when this reflection is recognized as operating with a peculiarly Western rather than transculturally available idiom, it begins to acquire some of the features of intratextuality.[20] In short, intratextuality may be a condition for the faithful description and development of a religion or tradition, but the material or doctrinal consequences of this self-evidently depend in part on what canon is appealed to.

It must also be noted that intratextuality in a postcritical or postliberal mode is significantly different from traditional precritical varieties. We now can make a distinction (unavailable before the development of modern science and historical studies) between realistic narrative and historical or scientific descriptions. The Bible is often "history-like" even when it is not "likely history." It can therefore be taken seriously in the first respect as a delineator of the character of divine and human agents, even when its history or science is challenged. As parables such as that of the prodigal son remind us, the rendering of God's character is not in every instance logically dependent on the facticity of the story.

Further, historical criticism influences the theological-literary interpretation of texts. A postcritical narrative reading of Scripture such as is found to some extent in von Rad's work on the Old Testament[21] is notably different from a precritical one. Or, to cite a more specific example, if the historical critic is right that the Johannine "Before Abraham was, I am" (John 8:58) is not a self-description of the preresurrection Jesus but a communal confession of faith, then even those who fully accept the confession will want to modify traditional theological descriptions of what Jesus was in his life on earth. They may agree doctrinally with Chalcedon, but prefer a Pauline *theologia crucis* to the Christological *theologia gloriae* that is often associated with Chalcedon (and that one finds even in great exponents of the theology of the cross such as Luther). Nevertheless, in an intratextual approach, literary considerations are more important than historical-critical ones in determining the canonical sense even in cases such as this. It is because the literary genre of John is clearly not that of veridical history that the statement in question can be readily accepted as a communal confession rather than a self-description.

Finally, and more generally, the postcritical focus on intratextual meanings does involve a change in attitude toward some aspects of the text that were important for premodern interpretation. The physical details of what, if anything, happened on Mt. Sinai, for example, are no longer of direct interest for typological or figurative purposes, as they often were for the tradition, but the basic questions remain much the same: What is the nature and function of Torah? It is in the New Testament custodial in Israel and fulfilled in Christ, but what does this imply for later Christianity and its relations to Judaism? Is not Torah by analogical extension both custodial and fulfilled for Christian communities in this age before the end when fulfillment is not yet final; and does this not make Christians much closer to Jews than they have generally thought? What, furthermore, does the Holocaust have to do with Mt. Sinai, on the one hand, and another mountain, Calvary, on the other? As these questions indicate, a postliberal intratextuality provides warrants for imaginatively and conceptually incorporating postbiblical worlds into the world of the Bible in much the same fashion as did the tradition. But the consequences inevitably will often be very different because of changes in the extrabiblical realities that are to be typologically interpreted and because of the more rigorous intratextuality made necessary by a critical approach to history.

In concluding this discussion, it needs to be reiterated that the practice of intratextuality is only loosely related to explicit theory. Just as good grammarians or mathematicians may be quite wrongheaded in their understanding of what they in fact actually do, so also with theologians. There is no reason for surprise if an apparent propositionalist, such as Aquinas, or an undoubted experiential-expressivist, such as Schleiermacher, were more intratextual in their actual practice than their theories would seem to allow. Their performance would perhaps have improved if their theories of religion had been different, but this is true only if other conditions remained equal. Native genius and religious commitment are helpful, but in order to convert these into theological competence one also needs a supportive environment, the tutelage of expert practitioners, and assiduous practice in a complex set of unformalizable skills that even the best theoretician cannot adequately characterize. Where these conditions are lacking, even good theory cannot greatly enhance performance, and where they are present, poor theory may be relatively harmless.

The implications of these observations do not bode well, however, for the future of postliberal theology. Even if it were to become theoretically popular, the result might chiefly be talk about intratextuality rather than more and better intratextual practice. The conditions for practice seem to be steadily weakening. Disarray in church and society makes the transmission of the necessary skills more and more difficult. Those who share in the intellectual high culture of our day are rarely intensively socialized into coherent religious languages and communal forms of life. This is not necessarily disastrous for the long-range prospects of religion (which is not dependent on elites), but it is for theology as an intellectually and academically creative enterprise capable of making significant contributions to the wider culture and society. Further, theology (in the sense of reflection in the service of religion) is being increasingly replaced in seminaries as well as universities by religious studies. There are fewer and fewer institutional settings favorable to the intratextual interpretation of religion and of extrascriptural realities.[22] Perhaps the last American theologian who in practice (and to some extent in theory) made extended and effective attempts to redescribe major aspects of the contemporary scene in distinctively Christian terms was Reinhold Niebuhr. After the brief neoorthodox interlude (which was itself sometimes thoroughly liberal in its theological methodology, as in the case of Paul Tillich), the liberal tendency to redescribe religion in extrascriptural frameworks has once again become dominant. This is understandable. Religions have become foreign texts that are much easier to translate into currently popular categories than to read in terms of their intrinsic sense. Thus the fundamental obstacles to intratextual theological faithfulness may well derive from the psychosocial situation rather than from scholarly or intellectual considerations.

III
APPLICABILITY AS FUTUROLOGY

We began this chapter by noting that theologies are assessed by their applicability as well as their faithfulness. They are judged by how relevant or practical they are in concrete situations as well as by how well they fit the cultural-linguistic systems whose religious uses they seek to describe. In this section we shall deal, first, with the relation of judgments of faithfulness and applicability and, second, with some specific issues that are of special concern today.

All-embracing systems of interpretation possess their own internal criteria of applicability: they can be judged by their own standards. This is evident when we consider how views of present practicality are shaped by visions of reality that encompass more than the present. A Marxist and a non-Marxist, for example, may agree in their factual descriptions of current trends and on the general principle that these trends should be evaluated in terms of long-range consequences, and yet they may differ sharply in their extrapolations. What seems to one the wave of the future will seem to the other a mere eddy in the river of time, and judgments of applicability or practicality will vary accordingly. The difference will be even greater if the non-Marxist is, for example, an Advaita Vedantist for whom the course of history is religiously irrelevant; but this kind of devaluation of the temporal future has not generally been characteristic of Western faiths.

Concern for the future has traditionally been associated in biblical religions with prophecy. Prophets proclaim what is both faithful and applicable in a given situation, and they oppose proposals that, whatever their apparent practicality, are doomed because of their unfaithfulness to God's future. To be sure, as biblical scholars remind us, prophetic utterances are not predictions in the ordinary sense. Jonah was disappointed by the non-fulfillment of his prophecies against Nineveh, but this did not make him doubt that God had spoken. The repentance that averted the destruction of the city was, so to speak, the point of the prophecy. Similarly, the nonfulfillment of expectations of an imminent Parousia have rarely been taken by those who shared them as evidence that Christ would not return. A similar logic operates in much nonreligious forecasting. The failure of Marxist and other secular anticipations of the early demise of religion does not disconfirm secularism, and the predictive inadequacies of contemporary futurology[23] have not discouraged its practitioners. In all these cases, the purpose is not to foretell what is to come, but to shape present action to fit the anticipated and hoped-for future.

Theological forms of this activity are more like contemporary futurology than biblical prophecy. Unlike prophecy, futurology does not depend on first-order inspiration or intuition, but is a second-order enterprise that draws on the full range of empirical studies in an effort to discover "the signs of the times."[24] As we have noted, these signs vary greatly from one overall pattern of interpretation to another—from, for example, Marxist to non-Marxist views. In the case of Christian theology, the purpose is to discern those possibilities in current situations that can and should be cultivated as anticipations or preparations for the hoped-for future, the coming kingdom. In brief, a theological proposal is adjudged both faithful and applicable to the degree that it appears practical in terms of an eschatologically and empirically defensible scenario of what is to come.

In the construction of such scenarios, the crucial difference between liberals and postliberals is in the way they correlate their visions of the future and of present situations. Liberals start with experience, with an account of the present, and then adjust their vision of the kingdom of God accordingly, while postliberals are in principle committed to doing the reverse. The first procedure makes it easier to accommodate to present trends, whether from the right or the left: Christian fellow travelers of both Nazism and Stalinism generally used liberal methodology to justify their positions. When, in contrast to this, one looks at the present in the light of an intratextually derived eschatology, one gets a different view of which contemporary developments are likely to be ultimately significant. Similar practical recommendations may at times be advanced, but for dissimilar theological reasons. A postliberal might argue, for example, that traditional sexual norms should be revised because the situation has changed from when they were formulated or because they are not intratextually faithful —but not, as some liberals may be inclined to argue, on the grounds that sexual liberation is an advance toward the eschatological future. Postliberalism is methodologically committed to neither traditionalism nor progressivism, but its resistance to current fashions, to making present experience revelatory, may often result in conservative stances. Yet there are numerous occasions in which the intratextual norm requires the rejection of the old in favor of the new.

These comments on method, however, leave untouched the question of the possible contemporary relevance of postliberalism. Earlier chapters suggested that a cultural-linguistic approach is supported by intellectual trends in nontheological disciplines, and that it can in its own way accommodate some of the main religious concerns that make experiential-expressivism appealing. Yet we also noted that the present psychosocial situation is more favorable to liberalism than to postliberalism. Sociologists have been telling us for a hundred years or more that the rationalization, pluralism, and mobility of modern life dissolve the bonds of tradition and community. This produces multitudes of men and women who are impelled, if they have religious yearnings, to embark on their own individual quests for symbols of transcendence. The churches have become purveyors of this commodity rather than communities that socialize their members into coherent and comprehensive religious outlooks and forms of life. Society paradoxically conditions human beings to experience selfhood as somehow prior to social influences, and Eastern religions and philosophies are utilized to support what, from a cultural-linguistic perspective, is the myth of the transcendental ego. Selfhood is experienced as a given rather than as either a gift or an achievement, and fulfillment comes from exfoliating or penetrating into the inner depths rather than from communally responsible action in the public world. Thus the cultural climate is on the whole antithetical to postliberalism.

One can argue, furthermore, that there is little likelihood that the cultural trends favoring experiential-expressivism will be reversed in the realistically forseeable future. If the nations are to avoid nuclear or environmental destruction, they will have to become ever more unified. What the world will need is some kind of highly generalized outlook capable of providing a framework for infinitely diversified religious quests. Experiential-expressivism with its openness to the hypothesis of an underlying unity can, it would seem, better fill this need than a cultural-linguistic understanding of religion with its stress on particularity. Western monotheisms especially appear to be disqualified because, on an intratextual reading, these religions cannot without suicide surrender their claims to the universal and unsurpassable validity of very specific identifications of the Ultimate with the God of Abraham, Isaac, and Jacob; of Jesus; or of the Koran. The future belongs, on this view, to liberal interpretations of religion.

In the speculative domain of futurology, however, it is easy to mount counterarguments. It can be pointed out that the indefinite extrapolation of present trends is a questionable procedure because any given tendency, if carried far enough, destroys the conditions for its own existence. When liberation from constraints produces chaos, the result is new bondage, and law and order are once again experienced as conditions for freedom. Law and order when unchecked, however, create rigidities that harbor the seeds of their own destruction. Similarly, the viability of a unified world of the future may well depend on counteracting the acids of modernity. It may depend on communal enclaves that socialize their members into highly particular outlooks supportive of concern for others rather than for individual rights and entitlements, and of a sense of responsibility for the wider society rather than for personal fulfillment. It is at least an open question whether any religion will have the requisite toughness for this demanding task unless it at some point makes the claim that it is significantly different and unsurpassably true; and it is easier for a religion to advance this claim if it is interpreted in cultural-linguistic rather than experiential-expressive terms. Thus it may well be that postliberal theologies are more applicable than liberal ones to the needs of the future.

These considerations gain in force when one considers what may be necessary for the viability, not of a world order, but of cultural traditions such as the Western one. If the Bible has shaped the imagination of the West to anywhere near the degree that Northrop Frye, for example, has argued,[25] then the West's continuing imaginative vitality and creativity may well depend on the existence of groups for whom the Hebrew and Christian Scriptures are not simply classics among others, but the canonical literature par excellence, and who are also in close contact with the wider culture. Much the same argument could be advanced in reference to the Koran and Islamic culture, and perhaps something analogous applies to the religions and cultures of the Far East despite their lack of equally well-defined preeminent canons. The general point is that, provided a religion stresses service rather than domination, it is likely to contribute more to the future of humanity if it preserves its own distinctiveness and integrity than if it yields to the homogenizing tendencies associated with liberal experiential-expressivism.

This conclusion is paradoxical: Religious communities are likely to be practically relevant in the long run to the degree that they do not first ask what is either practical or relevant, but instead concentrate on their own intratextual outlooks and forms of life. The much-debated problem of the relation of theory and praxis is thus dissolved by the communal analogue of justification by faith. As is true for individuals, so also a religious community's salvation is not by works, nor is its faith for the sake of practical efficacy, and yet good works of unforeseeable kinds flow from faithfulness. It was thus, rather than by intentional effort, that biblical religion helped produce democracy and science, as well as other values Westerners treasure; and it is in similarly unimaginable and unplanned ways, if at all, that biblical religion will help save the world (for Western civilization is now world civilization) from the demonic corruptions of these same values.

These arguments for the applicability of postliberal approaches cannot be neutrally evaluated. Those who think that religions are more the sources than the products of experience will regard a loss of religious particularity as impoverishing, while others will consider it enriching. Comprehensive frameworks of interpretation provide their own standards of relevance, and thus both liberal and postliberal outlooks have no difficulty in reading the signs of the times in such a way as to justify their own practicality.

IV
INTELLIGIBILITY AS SKILL

The case for applicability that has just been outlined is incomplete. It does not discuss whether postliberal theologies would help make religions more intelligible and credible. This is a practical as well as a theoretical question, and it can be formulated in terms of two closely related problems. First, intratextuality seems wholly relativistic: it turns religions, so one can argue, into self-enclosed and incommensurable intellectual ghettoes. Associated with this, in the second place, is the fideistic dilemma: it appears that choice between religions is purely arbitrary, a matter of blind faith.

These may not be mortal weaknesses in other times or places where communal traditions are relatively unbroken and faiths are transmitted from parents to children in successive generations, but they are, so it can be argued, obstacles to the survival of religions in pluralistic situations where religiousness usually involves decisions among competing alternatives. It seems essential in our day to adopt an apologetic approach that seeks to discover a foundational scheme within which religions can be evaluated, and that makes it possible to translate traditional meanings into currently intelligible terms. The postliberal resistance to the foundational enterprise is from this perspective a fatal flaw.

The great strength of theological liberalism, it can be argued, lies in its commitment to making religion experientially intelligible to the cultured and the uncultured among both its despisers and its appreciators. It is in order to clarify the gospel in a world where it has become opaque that liberals typically choose the categories in which to expound their systematic theologies; and it is by their success in communicating to the modern mind that they assess the faithfulness of their endeavors. This same concern accounts for the liberal commitment to the foundational enterprise of uncovering universal principles or structures—if not metaphysical, then existential, phenomenological, or hermeneutical. If there are no such universals, then how can one make the faith credible, not only to those outside the church but to the half-believers within it and, not least, to theologians? The liberal program is in one sense accommodation to culture, but it is often motivated by missionary impulses no less strong than those which send Wycliffe evangelicals overseas to translate the Bible into aboriginal tongues.

Postliberals are bound to be skeptical, not about missions, but about apologetics and foundations. To the degree that religions are like languages and cultures, they can no more be taught by means of translation than can Chinese or French. What is said in one idiom can to some extent be conveyed in a foreign tongue, but no one learns to understand and speak Chinese by simply hearing and reading translations. Resistance to translation does not wholly exclude apologetics, but this must be of an ad hoc and nonfoundational variety rather than standing at the center of theology. The grammar of religion, like that of language, cannot be explicated or learned by analysis of experience, but only by practice. Religious and linguistic competence may help greatly in dealing with experience, but experience by itself may be more a hindrance than a help to acquiring competence: children, at least in Jesus' parabolic sense, have an advantage over adults. In short, religions, like languages, can be understood only in their own terms, not by transposing them into an alien speech.

Yet this approach, as was noted in earlier chapters, need not confine the theological study of religion to an intellectual ghetto, but can free it for closer contact with other disciplines. The spread of a cultural-linguistic orientation in history, anthropology, sociology, and philosophy increases interest in intratextuality, in the description of religions from the inside. Liberal attempts to explain religions by translating them into other conceptualities seem to appeal chiefly to theologians or to other religious people.

As modern culture moves ever farther away from its religious roots, these translations become more strained, complex, and obscure to the uninitiated. Relativism increases and foundational appeals to universal structures of thought, experience, or *Existenz* lose their persuasiveness. Tillich communicated to a wide range of intellectuals a generation ago, but it is doubtful that his numerous liberal successors could now match his record even if they had his talent. Scholarly nontheologians who want to understand religion are concerned with how religions work for their adherents, not with their credibility. Their interest, one might say, is in descriptive rather than apologetic intelligibility. The result, paradoxically, is that a postliberal approach, with its commitment to intratextual description, may well have interdisciplinary advantages, while liberal theology, with its apologetic focus on making religion more widely credible, seems increasingly to be a nineteenth-century enclave in a twentieth-century milieu.

These considerations, however, leave unresolved the problem with which we started this section. The question is whether intratextual descriptive intelligibility is helpful for religious and not simply interdisciplinary purposes; but if intratextuality implies relativism and fideism, the cost for most religious traditions is much too high. If there are no universal or foundational structures and standards of judgment by which one can decide between different religious and nonreligious options, the choice of any one of them becomes, it would seem, purely irrational, a matter of arbitrary whim or blind faith; and while this conclusion may fit much of the modern mood, it is antithetical to what most religions, whether interpreted in liberal, preliberal, or postliberal fashion, have affirmed.

Antifoundationalism, however, is not to be equated with irrationalism. The issue is not whether there are universal norms of reasonableness, but whether these can be formulated in some neutral, framework-independent language.[26] Increasing awareness of how standards of rationality vary from field to field and age to age makes the discovery of such a language more and more unlikely and the possibility of foundational disciplines doubtful. Yet this does not reduce the choice between different frameworks to whim or chance. As T. S. Kuhn has argued in reference to science, and Wittgenstein in philosophy, the norms of reasonableness are too rich and subtle to be adequately specified in any general theory of reason or knowledge. These norms, to repeat a point often made in this book, are like the rules of depth grammar, which linguists search for and may at times approximate but never grasp. Thus reasonableness in religion and theology, as in other domains, has something of that aesthetic character, that quality of unformalizable skill, which we usually associate with the artist or the linguistically competent. If so, basic religious and theological positions, like Kuhn's scientific paradigms, are invulnerable to definitive refutation (as well as confirmation) but can nevertheless be tested and argued about in various ways, and these tests and arguments in the long run make a difference. Reason places constraints on religious as well as on scientific options even though these constraints are too flexible and informal to be spelled out in either foundational theology or a general theory of science. In short, intelligibility comes from skill, not theory, and credibility comes from good performance, not adherence to independently formulated criteria.

In this perspective, the reasonableness of a religion is largely a function of its assimilative powers, of its ability to provide an intelligible interpretation in its own terms of the varied situations and realities adherents encounter.[27] The religions we call primitive regularly fail this test when confronted with major changes, while the world religions have developed greater resources for coping with vicissitude. Thus, although a religion is not susceptible to decisive disproof, it is subject, as Basil Mitchell argues,[28] to rational testing procedures not wholly unlike those which apply to general scientific theories or paradigms (for which, unlike hypotheses, there are no crucial experiments). Confirmation or disconfirmation occurs through an accumulation of successes or failures in making practically and cognitively coherent sense of relevant data, and the process does not conclude, in the case of religions, until the disappearance of the last communities of believers or, if the faith survives, until the end of history. This process certainly does not enable individuals to decide between major alternatives on the basis of reason alone, but it does provide warrants for taking reasonableness in religion seriously, and it helps explain why the intellectual labors of theologians, though vacuous without corresponding practice, do sometimes make significant contributions to the health of religious traditions.

Most premodern theological views of the relation of faith and reason are consistent with this outlook. Even Luther's attacks on "whore reason" are not fideistic: he affirms the importance of reason (at times including scholastic logic) in expounding Christian truth against both heretics and pagans.[29] On the other end of the spectrum, Aquinas' use of reason does not lead to foundational or natural theology of the modern type. Even when he is most the apologist, as in demonstrating the existence of God, his proofs are, by his own account, "probable arguments" in support of faith rather than parts of an independent foundational enterprise.[30] Both these thinkers, despite their material differences, can be viewed as holding that revelation dominates all aspects of the theological enterprise, but without excluding a subsidiary use of philosophical and experiential considerations in the explication and defense of the faith. Similarly, a postliberal approach need not exclude an ad hoc apologetics, but only one that is systematically prior and controlling in the fashion of post-Cartesian natural theology and of later liberalism. As Aquinas himself notes, reasoning in support of the faith is not meritorious before faith, but only afterward;[31] or, in the conceptuality employed in this book, the logic of coming to believe, because it is like that of learning a language, has little room for argument, but once one has learned to speak the language of faith, argument becomes possible.

Yet, though postliberal antifoundationalism need not imply relativism or fideism, the question remains of how to exhibit the intelligibility and possible truth of the religious message to those who no longer understand the traditional words. How, as modern Christians often put it, does one preach the gospel in a dechristianized world? Those for whom this problem is theologically primary regularly become liberal foundationalists. The first task of the theologian, they argue, is to identify the modern questions that must be addressed, and then to translate the gospel answers into a currently understandable conceptuality. If this is not done, the message will fall on deaf ears inside as well as outside the church; and unless postliberal theology has some way of meeting this need, it will be adjudged faithless and inapplicable as well as unintelligible by the religious community.

The postliberal method of dealing with this problem is bound to be unpopular among those chiefly concerned to maintain or increase the membership and influence of the church. This method resembles ancient catechesis more than modern translation.[32] Instead of redescribing the faith in new concepts, it seeks to teach the language and practices of the religion to potential adherents. This has been the primary way of transmitting the faith and winning converts for most religions down through the centuries. In the early days of the Christian church, for example, it was the gnostics, not the catholics, who were most inclined to redescribe the biblical materials in a new interpretive framework. Pagan converts to the catholic mainstream did not, for the most part, first understand the faith and then decide to become Christians; rather, the process was reversed: they first decided and then they understood. More precisely, they were first attracted by the Christian community and form of life. The reasons for attraction ranged from the noble to the ignoble and were as diverse as the individuals involved; but for whatever motives, they submitted themselves to prolonged catechetical instruction in which they practiced new modes of behavior and learned the stories of Israel and their fulfillment in Christ. Only after they had acquired proficiency in the alien Christian language and form of life were they deemed able intelligently and responsibly to profess the faith, to be baptized.

Later, when Christianity became socially dominant, this kind of catechesis disappeared, but similar results were obtained, though in diluted form, through the normal processes of maturation. In both cases, whether through catechesis or socialization, an intimate and imaginatively vivid familiarity with the world of biblical narrative was produced that made it possible to experience the whole of life in religious terms. The popular versions of the biblical world may often have been gravely distorted, but they functioned intratextually.

Western culture is now at an intermediate stage, however, where socialization is ineffective, catechesis impossible, and translation a tempting alternative. The biblical heritage continues to be powerfully present in latent and detextualized forms that immunize against catechesis but invite redescription. There is often enough Christian substance remaining to make the redescriptions meaningful. Marxism, as is often noted, is a secularized form of biblical eschatology, and existentialism and depth psychology develop themes from Reformation anthropology divorced from Reformation theology.[33] The experience and self-identity of even the unchurched masses remain deeply influenced by the religious past. They often insist to sociological investigators, for example, that they are just as genuinely Christian as the pious folk who go to church; and they sometimes make this claim, interestingly enough, even when they deny life after death and consider the existence of a creator God unlikely. Jesus Christ is not the Son of God for them, and their picture of him may be drastically unscriptural, but his name is part of their being.[34] They are immunized against catechesis, but are sometimes interested in translations of the gospel into existential, depth-psychological, or liberationist language that articulates their latent Christianity.

The impossibility of effective catechesis in the present situation is partly the result of the implicit assumption that knowledge of a few tag ends of religious language is knowledge of the religion (although no one would make this assumption about Latin). More important, however, is the character of churches during times of progressive dechristianization. In the present situation, unlike periods of missionary expansion, the churches primarily accommodate to the prevailing culture rather than shape it. Presumably they cannot do otherwise. They continue to embrace in one fashion or another the majority of the population and must cater willy-nilly to majority trends. This makes it difficult for them to attract assiduous catechumens even from among their own children, and when they do, they generally prove wholly incapable of providing effective instruction in distinctively Christian language and practice. Those who are looking for alternatives to, for example, the American way of life turn instead to Eastern religions or to deviant offshoots of the Christian mainstream. This situation is not likely to change until dechristianization has proceeded much farther or, less plausibly, is fundamentally reversed.

When or if dechristianization reduces Christians to a small minority, they will need for the sake of survival to form communities that strive without traditionalist rigidity to cultivate their native tongue and learn to act accordingly. Until that happens, however, catechetical methods of communicating the faith are likely to be unemployable in mainstream Christianity. The by no means illegitimate desire of the churches to maintain membership and of theologians to make the faith credible, not least to themselves, will continue to favor experiential-expressive translations into contemporary idioms.

CONCLUSION

This chapter ends on an inconclusive note. Postliberal theologies employing a cultural-linguistic understanding of religion can be faithful, applicable, and intelligible. There is thus no theological, just as there is no doctrinal, reason for rejecting them. Yet the intratextual intelligibility that postliberalism emphasizes may not fit the needs of religions such as Christianity when they are in the awkwardly intermediate stage of having once been culturally established but are not yet clearly disestablished.

Those of postliberal inclinations will be undeterred. They will argue for intratextuality on both religious and nonreligious grounds: the integrity of the faith demands it, and the vitality of Western societies may well depend in the long run on the culture-forming power of the biblical outlook in its intratextual, untranslatable specificity. Theology should therefore resist the clamor of the religiously interested public for what is currently fashionable and immediately intelligible. It should instead prepare for a future when continuing dechristianization will make greater Christian authenticity communally possible.

Those who hold that religious faithfulness is first of all the presentation of the religious message in currently intelligible forms will, of course, disagree. Their liberal premise, furthermore, can be canonically defended. There is much in Scripture and tradition to suggest that preaching the gospel understandably is a necessary part of faithfulness. In short, as was said at the beginning of this chapter, the case for the theological viability of a cultural-linguistic view of religion can only be presented, not proved. Field-encompassing interpretive frameworks shape their own criteria of adequacy.

The ultimate test in this as in other areas is performance. If a postliberal approach in its actual employment proves to be conceptually powerful and practically useful to the relevant communities, it will in time become standard. It was thus that the theological outlooks of Augustine, Aquinas, Luther, and Schleiermacher established themselves. There is no way of testing the merits and demerits of a theological method apart from performance.

The present chapter, however, is not a theological performance but at most a fragment of ad hoc apologetics. It discusses theology, but there is, by intratextual standards, scarcely a single properly theological argument in it. Such arguments in defense of its theses can, I think, be found in sources as diverse as Aquinas, the Reformers, and Karl Barth, but these have simply been mentioned, not deployed.

Yet, like most programmatic proposals, the present one is not simply an invitation to future work but is also dependent on past performances. The reader will recall that the stimulus for this book comes from the conviction that the doctrinal results of the ecumenical discussions of the last decades make better sense in the context of a cultural-linguistic view of religion and a rule theory of doctrine than in any other framework. Like the subjects of the Postman-Bruner card experiment mentioned in the Foreword, I have repeatedly had the experience of seeing that old categories (such as propositional or symbolic construals of doctrine) simply do not apply to what is now happening, but that light dawns when one uses a new category (church doctrines as instantiations of regulative principles within a cultural-linguistic system). Further, on the specifically theological side, Karl Barth's exegetical emphasis on narrative has been at second hand[35] a chief source of my notion of intratextuality as an appropriate way of doing theology in a fashion consistent with a cultural-linguistic understanding of religion and a regulative view of doctrine.

It remains an open question, however, whether the intratextual path will be pursued. There is much talk at present about typological, figurative, and narrative theology, but little actual performance. Only in some younger theologians does one see the beginnings of a desire to renew in a posttraditional and postliberal mode the ancient practice of absorbing the universe into the biblical world. May their tribe increase.

NOTES

1. The type of theology I have in mind could also be called "postmodern," "postrevisionist," or "post-neo-orthodox," but "postliberal" seems best because what I have in mind postdates the experiential-expressive approach which is the mark of liberal method. This technical use of the word is much broader than the ordinary one: methodological liberals may be conservative or traditionalist in theology and reactionary in social or political matters (as the reference, on p. 126 of this chapter, to the pro-Nazi *Deutsche Christen* is meant to indicate).

2. Clifford Geertz, *The Interpretation of Cultures* (Basic Books, 1973), pp. 3–30.

The quotations that follow in this paragraph are taken in order from pp. 17, 21, 13, 10, and 26.

3. E. E. Evans-Pritchard, *Nuer Religion* (Oxford: Oxford University Press, 1956), p. 84. This "notorious ethnographic example" is cited by T. M. S. Evans, "On the Social Anthropology of Religions," *Journal of Religion,* 62/4 (1982), p. 376.

4. Unlike David Tracy, *The Analogical Imagination* (Crossroad Publishing Co., 1981), I am using "classic" to refer to texts that are culturally established for whatever reason. Tracy's model, in contrast to mine, is experiential-expressive. For him classics are "certain expressions of the human spirit [which] so disclose a compelling truth about our lives that we cannot deny them some kind of normative status" (p. 108).

5. This and the following descriptions of intratextuality were composed without conscious reference to deconstructionism, but, given the current prominence of this form of literary theory, some tentative comments on similarities and dissimilarities may be desirable in order to avoid misunderstandings. First, intratextualism, like deconstructionism, does not share the traditional literary emphasis on a text as that which is to be interpreted, whether (as in the now-old "New Criticism") as a self-contained aesthetic object or "verbal icon," or as mimetic, or as expressive, or as pragmatic. (For the meaning of these terms, see Meyer H. Abrams, *The Mirror and the Lamp: Romantic Theory and the Critical Tradition* [Oxford: Oxford University Press, 1953]; cited by M. A. Tolbert, *Religious Study Review* 8/1 [1982], p. 2.) Instead, intratextualism treats texts—to use a phrase applied to languages in earlier chapters—as "mediums of interpretation," and thus shares the deconstructionist emphasis on texts as constituting the (or a) world within which everything is or can be construed. Related to this, in the second place, is a common concern (as will later become apparent) with what Christopher Norris, speaking of Paul de Man, calls "the play of figural language," "the grammar of tropes," and "the rhetoric of textual performance." (Christopher Norris, *Deconstruction: Theory and Practise* [Methuen & Co., 1982], pp. 106, 108.) In the third place, however, the great difference is that for the deconstructionists there is no single privileged idiom, text, or text-constituted world. Their approach is *inter*textual rather than intratextual—that is, they treat all writings as a single whole: all texts are, so to speak, mutually interpreting. One result is that what in the past would have been thought of as allegorizing is for them an acceptable mode of interpretation. In an intratextual religious or theological reading, in contrast, there is (as this chapter later notes at length) a privileged interpretive direction from whatever counts as holy writ to everything else. Other differences as well as similarities are discussed by Shira Wolosky in a treatment of Derrida's relation to Talmudic modes of interpretation ("Derrida, Jabes, Levinas: Sign Theory as Ethical Discourse," *Journal of Jewish Literary History* 2/3 [1982], pp. 283–301). It should incidentally be noted, however, that Derrida's understanding of Christian interpretive method as presented in this article is quite different from the typological approach, which I shall argue was historically dominant. It may be that Derrida's view of what is characteristically Christian in these matters has been influenced by the experiential-expressive hermeneutics of Paul Ricoeur, whose student he once was.

6. Thomas Aquinas, *ST* I.1.10.

7. For the structure, though not all the details, of my understanding of typological interpretation, see Hans Frei, *The Eclipse of Biblical Narrative* (Yale University Press, 1974), esp. pp. 1–39.

8. Charles Wood, *The Formation of Christian Understanding* (Westminster Press, 1981), pp. 42, 101, and passim.

9. See my review of Gerhard Ebeling's *Dogmatik des Christlichen Glaubens,* in *Journal of Religion* 61 (1981), pp. 309–314.

10. Frei, *The Eclipse of Biblical Narrative,* pp. 39ff.

11. For the general way of looking at the problem of scriptural interpretation presented in this paragraph, though not for all the details, I am indebted to David Kelsey, *The Uses of Scripture in Recent Theology* (Fortress Press, 1975).

12. This way of putting the matter is dependent on Hans Frei, *The Identity of Jesus Christ* (Fortress Press, 1975).

13. In addition to Hans Küng's *On Being a Christian* (tr. by Edward Quinn [Doubleday & Co., 1976]), see his "Toward a New Consensus in Catholic (and Ecumenical) Theology," in Leonard Swidler (ed.), *Consensus in Theology?* (Westminster Press, 1980), pp. 1–17.

14. This is the focus of attack in Hick (ed.), *The Myth of God Incarnate* (Westminster Press, 1977). See Chapter 5, n. 1, above.

15. Edward Schillebeeckx, *Jesus: An Experiment in Christology,* tr. by Hubert Hoskins (Seabury Press, 1979).

16. David Tracy, *Blessed Rage for Order* (Seabury Press, 1975).

17. Karl Barth's way of doing this is described and critically but sympathetically assessed in David Ford, *Barth and God's Story* (Frankfurt: Peter Lang, 1981). See also D. Ford, "Narrative in Theology," *British Journal of Religious Education* 4/3 (1982), pp. 115–119.

18. David Kelsey, *The Uses of Scripture in Recent Theology,* p. 48.

19. Ibid.

20. Richard Rorty partly illustrates this possibility of doing philosophy intratextually, but the inevitable vagueness of his canon of philosophical texts makes him verge on a philosophical version of deconstructionism. See his *Consequences of Pragmatism* (University of Minnesota Press, 1982), esp. essays 6 (on Derrida), 8, and 12, and the Introduction.

21. Gerhard von Rad, *Old Testament Theology,* tr. by D. M. G. Stalker, 2 vols. (Harper & Row, 1962, 1965).

22. See Chapter 1, n. 30, above.

23. For example, the pioneering work *Toward the Year 2000,* ed. by Daniel Bell (Beacon Press, 1969), now seems extraordinarily dated.

24. My own two minor exercises in this genre (see Chapter 1, n. 22, above) are basic to the following paragraphs.

25. Northrop Frye, *The Great Code: The Bible and Literature* (Harcourt Brace Jovanovich, 1982).

26. For the argument of this paragraph, see George Lindbeck, "Theologische Methode und Wissenschaftstheorie," *Theologische Revue* 74 (1978), pp. 267–280.

This article has not been published in English. See also Chapter 3, section IV, above, for a discussion of the status of religious truth claims.

27. What I have in mind here might be called "assimilation by interpretation" and is to be distinguished from what Cardinal Newman, using the same name, listed as the third mark of authentic doctrinal development. The analogies he used were organic, not interpretive: for example, a plant assimilates foreign material from its environment. (John Henry Newman, *An Essay on the Development of Christian Doctrine* [Doubleday & Co., Image Books, 1960], pp. 189–192, 338–360.)

28. Basil Mitchell, *The Justification of Religious Belief* (London: Macmillan & Co., 1973).

29. Brian Gerrish, *Grace and Reason: A Study in the Theology of Luther* (Oxford: Oxford University Press, 1962), esp. pp. 168–171; Philip Watson, *Let God Be God! An Interpretation of the Theology of Martin Luther* (Muhlenberg Press, 1947), pp. 73ff.

30. Thomas Aquinas, *ST* I.1.8, ad 2.

31. Ibid., II–II.2.10.

32. Cf. n. 26, above.

33. See article cited in Chapter 4, n. 17, above.

34. Such attitudes are also widespread in Europe, where church attendance is much smaller than in the United States. See H. Hild (ed.), *Wie stabil ist die Kirche? Bestand und Erneuerung: Ergebnisse einer Meinungsbefragung* (Gelnhausen: Burck-hardthaus-Verlag, 1974). See also Gerhard Szczesny, "Warum ich als Nichtchrist Weihnachten feiere," in H. Nitschke (ed.), *Was fällt ihnen zu Weihnachten ein?* (Gütersloh: Gütersloher Verlagshaus Gerd Mohn, 1978), pp. 50ff.

35. Cf. Kelsey, *The Uses of Scripture in Recent Theology,* pp. 39–50 and passim; also Ford, *Barth and God's Story;* but I have learned to think about Barth in this way above all from conversations with Hans Frei.

INDEX